Praise for *On Chapel Sands*

An NPR Best Book of the Year
Finalist for a National Book Critics Circle Award
Shortlisted for the Costa Biography Award
Shortlisted for the Baillie Gifford Prize for Non-Fiction
Shortlisted for the Rathbones Folio Prize
Longlisted for the RSL Ondaatje Prize

"Vivid . . . Cumming, an art critic, anchors her story to references from art and literature, exploring the shaping of identity and what makes us 'belong' to the people and places that call us their own."

—*The New Yorker*

"One of the most compelling memoirs of recent years, a book with as many twists and turns as any mystery, a family history of great emotional resonance . . . It's an extraordinary story, and an even better book."

—*Los Angeles Times*

"Reads like a thriller . . . Questions and lies abound in this touching book about a daughter's quest to help her aging mother uncover her true identity."

—*Publishers Weekly*

"A satisfying mystery that could have been grist for Agatha Christie's mill. [Cumming's] nuanced, pensive account restores reality and

vitality to figures from out of the past, making them meaningful while uncovering their secrets."

—*Kirkus Reviews*

"How we see—and who see and what secrets they choose to share—is at the heart of this exquisitely composed memoir. . . . A peerless detective story that keeps you guessing to the end."

—*The Sunday Times* (UK), "Memoir of the Year"

"Brilliant . . . Cumming is adept in knowing how much to disclose and when to hold back. . . . The book is a love letter to her mother, whose warmth, articulacy, and survival instincts shine through."

—*The Guardian* (UK)

"A literary whodunit that is both page-turning and richly absorbing. . . . Her story is a triumph of the human spirit, and Cumming tells it with a researcher's meticulous care and a novelist's keen sense of character."

—*Providence Journal*

"This is an incredible, and incredibly unusual, book about family, secrets, the ruinous sexual shame and hypocrisy of the first half of the English twentieth century. It's one of the best memoirs I have ever read. . . . There is so much about *On Chapel Sands* that moves; there is so much about it that educates. It is, and will remain, a favorite, to be re-read one day, to be recommended to anyone who will listen."

—Nick Hornby, *The Believer*

"By turns beautiful, wistful, and ominous . . . the reasons behind the kidnapping, and the repercussions, are every bit as complex as any served up by fiction, and, oddly enough, the dénouement—or succession of dénouements—is just as satisfying, perhaps more so. . . . [A] meditation on the way some people disappear and time erases memory . . . so familiar as to be universal."

—*Daily Mail* (UK)

"An outstanding achievement . . . Much more than a search for truth. It is a moving, many-sided human story of great depth and tenderness, and a revelation of how art enriches life. In short, a masterpiece."

—*The Sunday Times* (UK)

"Illuminating and deeply touching . . . [A]t its heart is Cumming's belief in interpretation as a process of understanding, not just of art but of our lives and actions."

—*The Spectator* (UK)

"A story told with such depth of feeling and observation and such lyrical writing that I have been unable to put it down. . . . Cumming is an art critic, and in this book she has created a great mural of words, filled with people so tangible you almost expect them to swivel on the page and look at you. And the great mystery turns out to be, not what happened on that beach to one little girl, but how all of us sometimes stumble, sometimes soar, through courage, strength, and love."

—Anna Quindlen, author of *Miller's Valley*

ALSO BY LAURA CUMMING

The Vanishing Velázquez
A Face to the World: On Self-Portraits

ON CHAPEL SANDS

The Mystery of My Mother's
Disappearance as a Child

LAURA CUMMING

SCRIBNER

NEW YORK   LONDON   TORONTO   SYDNEY   NEW DELHI

Scribner
An Imprint of Simon & Schuster, Inc.
1230 Avenue of the Americas
New York, NY 10020

First Scribner trade paperback edition February 2021

SCRIBNER and design are registered trademarks of The Gale Group, Inc.,
used under license by Simon & Schuster, Inc., the publisher of this work.

For information about special discounts for bulk purchases,
please contact Simon & Schuster Special Sales at 1-866-506-1949
or business@simonandschuster.com.

The Simon & Schuster Speakers Bureau can bring authors to your live event.
For more information or to book an event, contact the Simon & Schuster Speakers Bureau
at 1-866-248-3049 or visit our website at www.simonspeakers.com.

Manufactured in the United States of America

1 3 5 7 9 10 8 6 4 2

Library of Congress Control Number: 2019943700

ISBN 978-1-5011-9871-7
ISBN 978-1-5011-9872-4 (pbk)
ISBN 978-1-5011-9873-1 (ebook)

For my beloved mother and daughters
Elizabeth, Hilla, and Thea
and in memory of Veda, Hilda, and George

An Hour is a Sea
Between a few, and me—
With them would Harbor be—

Emily Dickinson

All the characters and events in this book are real.
Only one name has been changed,
in the final chapter.

CONTENTS

ON CHAPEL
SANDS

I

The Beach

This is how it began, and how it would end, on the long pale strand of a Lincolnshire beach in the last hour of sun, the daylight moon small as a kite in the sky. Far below, a child of three was playing by herself with a new tin spade. It was still strangely warm in that autumn of 1929, and she had taken off her plimsolls to feel the day's heat lingering in the sand beneath her feet. Short fair hair, no coat, blue eyes and dress to match: that was the description later given to the police.

She had come out of the house that afternoon and along the short path to the beach with her mother, Mrs. Veda Elston. They had already been there for some time, with biscuits in an old tartan tin, digging and sieving the sand. The tide was receding when they arrived, the concussion of waves on the shore gradually quieting as the day wore on; by now the sea was almost half a mile in the distance. In this lull, on their own familiar beach, and so comfortingly close to home, Veda must have let her daughter wander free for a moment. For she did not see what happened next.

Someone moved swiftly across the beach and began talking to the little girl. Someone she perhaps knew, because no sounds were heard as they coaxed her away. One minute she was there, barefoot and absorbed, spade in hand; seconds later she was taken off the sands at the village of Chapel St. Leonards, apparently without anybody noticing at all. Thus was my mother kidnapped.

I see the scene again and again, always trying to grasp the unfathomable moment in which she vanished and everything changed. The place where she was playing empties into air; the tide freezes; the beach turns blank. Time stands still on the shore. How many minutes before her absence begins to register, before Veda becomes uneasy and then fearful, before the silence is broken by shouting and rushing to the spot where the spade lies fallen? The waves continue their impervious lapping, gulls drifting on the surface as the afternoon fades. How long before anybody missed my mother?

* * *

I have the police report of that day. It is scant. Mrs. Elston takes her daughter to the beach at or around 2:30 p.m. Approximately two hours later, the child disappears so fast that she couldn't have got anywhere near the water. Unable to find her on the sands, Mrs. Elston retraces their steps, searching the path and even the house in case she might have found her way home. Neighbors help look for the child. An urgent telegram is sent to the father, who is away for work, summoning him back to Chapel.

All of this is duly reported to the police, but not until the following day; and not, I suspect, by Veda. I hear instead the brusque authority of my grandfather George. Veda appears silent with shock. All she offers, via her husband, is the possibility that the child must have wandered up the beach behind her and out of sight. She herself was sitting on a blanket, knitting or staring dreamily out to sea in the mild afternoon sun, as I imagine it, with one eye on the child, occasionally plying her with biscuits—until she just slipped out of view. Perhaps the crisis was not immediately apparent. After all, the beach at Chapel was so innocent, like the child, and her little legs could not have carried her far. But then came darkness with no trace, and more stricken searching, before Veda had to spend the first dreadful night alone without her daughter.

How could she have disappeared? The beach, to begin with, is completely flat. A broad street of spotless sand, scattered with angel-wing shells, it seems to stretch forever in both directions. There are no coves, dunes, or rocks where an adult could hide a child; everything stands in open view.

To reach it you must walk up and over an artificial incline of heaped sand that is supposed to act as a barrier to the sea; a barrier so ineffectual that houses, cattle, and villagers have been swept away in historic storms. This little embankment runs for miles along the coastline, and from its top people can be seen walking far away in the distance. Tennyson, the Victorian poet born and raised not far from Chapel, was drawn back to it all through his life. "I used to stand on this sand-built ridge," he wrote in old age, "and think it was the spine-bone of the world!"

Veda's mother once saw Tennyson on Chapel Sands: pressing along against the strident northeasterly winds, black cloak blowing, hat held on in brows-down melancholy.

Come over this ridge, and even more surprising than the flatness is the way the sand appears to merge with the sea. The beach is tawny brown and so is the brine, because it washes over beds of clay. On a still day they become one vast continuous expanse, an optical illusion only dispelled when a chink of reflected blue sky spangles the water or a sudden gust troubles the surface.

Perhaps that stillness slowed the events of the day. Veda did not notice what was happening quickly enough. Nobody scrambled up that ridge in time to spot any hurriedly departing figures. Footsteps muffled by the sand, voices dispersed on the mellow sea air, all it took was a prolonged moment of parental inattention. No commotion. Nobody saw, and perhaps there were few other people there to witness the incident, for it was a weekday afternoon in October. Nor was this yet a crowded beach as it is today in high season. Black-and-white photographs from the 1920s show deserted sands or very occasional hikers in hobnail boots and straw hats buying tea from a hut by the Pulley, as they still call the narrow passage where horses once pulled cargoes of tobacco and paraffin over the ridge into the village.

The beach was always Chapel's livelihood. Boats went out for whiting, people searched for mussels and shrimped in the waves at low tide. Ships sometimes ran aground, stalled in the shallows, their debris washing fruitfully ashore. There might be wood for the fire, treasurable in those days before electricity; and on Sundays people took bags and went coaling. Stranger things turned up too. A ship running guns lost its dangerous cargo at Chapel and soldiers had to be brought in to handle the live ammunition. A case of glassware was shared out among the villagers, not a single piece shattered. And once a crate of grapefruit spilled out across the sands, odd yellow globes never seen before by anyone except Mr. Stow, proprietor of Stow's Stores by the Pulley; where in the world had they come from?

All along the sea's margin, curds of delicate foam arrive on incoming waves. My mother used to hurl them gleefully about, risking her father's instant reproach. In winter, sea-driven winds direct from Scandinavia skim sand into the air, stinging the eyes and gritting the mouth. There are spring tides when the water feels warmer than the gray rain spattering its surface, and blazing summer days when you can swim forever, it feels, along the unchanging shore. This level strand, with its inviting sea, was the great playground of my mother's youth. She went there with George, paddling in the shallow froth, clambering about the tide pools, digging holes, drawing in the sand. He took photographs of her with his Box Brownie, and even in those monochrome days they show the beach at Chapel exactly as I knew it too, from the holidays of my own childhood.

Photography gives us memories we hardly knew we had: the house where we were born, our infant selves, the embarrassing clothes we once wore. But the camera is also capable of giving us memories we cannot actually have because we were not there in the first place. This rare gift, this strange illusion of déjà vu, characterizes all of George's pictures for me. He photographs his daughter on the shore, laughing in a swimming costume I remember as pale

lilac, embroidered with a butterfly, though of course I neither saw nor wore it. She sits in front of a bell tent with a kettle brewing on a portable stove, its meager flame the result of the purple methylated spirits that fueled it, and I scent that sharp stinging reek. There is a picture of her beaming at the bottom of a gigantic hole which I know George has been excavating all day, the sand damper and colder the deeper he digs into the secret innards of the beach. She is carefully seated inside, in clean clothes for the camera. I am with her, smile pinned to my face too, waiting to be lifted back out.

Every beach shot is ecstatic, and almost proverbial: my mother looks happy as a clam. Years of happiness, or so it seems, on Chapel Sands. I particularly love the sight of her perched on the shoulders of a sun-browned man who bears his load with patient resignation.

She is about five, so tanned her eyebrows look white, and the lilac costume is nearly slipping from her thin body as she lifts her arms like a gleeful reveler at a festival. The man's name is Frank, and he is a friend of George, who is in his customary position behind the camera. But a line of apparently innocuous foam is stealing up behind them. Not many weeks after the picture was taken, Frank fell deeply asleep on an inflatable raft on this beach. The tide stole him away to his fate, a dark disappearance somewhere out in the North Sea.

All the beach photographs in the Elston family album were

taken by George. He would not yield his Box Brownie to anyone else, which is why he never appears on the shore with his daughter. But on the other hand, neither does Veda. I did not notice these absences as a child, leafing through the illuminated treasury of my mother's early life, images to go with the stories she told, but of course they strike me every time I look as an adult. George Elston is there, recording the moment, but his wife is not. My mother has not a single memory of going to the beach again with Veda.

The photographs in the family album are few and tiny, no larger than a matchbox, in a landscape-shaped book that is barely ten inches by eight. This modest volume has only twenty-two pages, yet half of them are completely empty. All my life this puzzled me. For years I thought it was a matter of thrift; but film for a Box Brownie was relatively cheap, even for a poor family like the Elstons. In fact, George appears to be selecting only the best images from many rolls of film for his album; there are rejects in the back, and considerable time passes between one picture and the next. And time is precisely what I should have noticed. There are no photographs of my mother before the age of three. There are none of Veda, George, and Betty together, and the whole narrative runs out when she is around the age of thirteen. One decade in the light, then many black pages.

"Betty, Chapel." This is written in George's firm hand on the back of these photographs of his daughter. Other people drift in and out of shot, nameless strangers, now forgotten. But she is always given as Betty. Except in one stray image, slipped inside the back cover of the album, never attached, that does not fit anywhere in the sequence. This picture shows my mother as a young child on Chapel Sands, but with a different name on the reverse in an unknown hand. Here she is not called Betty. She is Grace.

My mother was born in August 1926 in the shadow of a windmill in a Lincolnshire village. One month later, she was christened Grace in the parish church. No father is cited on the birth certificate; the child was to be considered fatherless. At the age of three, she was passed to George and Veda Elston, given this new name Betty, and taken to live in Chapel St. Leonards. The Elstons were going to be her parents now. Henceforth, she was to be considered lucky.

But she did not feel that way. As an adult she began to call herself Elizabeth, having always hated the name Betty, specifically for its associations with George. It was incredible to me, when young, that this abundantly loving woman could have so loathed her father that she would change her own name to be free of his reach. But I knew very little of her story yet, and neither did she. My mother did not see her own birth certificate until she was forty. She did not know that she was once called Grace, had no sense of her existence before the age of three. The knowledge of her early life came—and went—in waves over the years. Something would be established, believed, and then washed away; then it would happen all over again, the arriving wave disrupting the old in a kind of tidal confusion. Even now, in her nineties, she has no idea precisely how or why she ceased to be Grace, but I know that it was before she ever reached the home of Veda and George. She stopped searching long ago, but now I must discover the truth of her story.

The name they will be calling in desperation on the sands that day is Betty—Betty Elston, three-year-old daughter of the Elstons at Number 1 St. Leonard's Villas, who are well known in Chapel. George Maybrook Elston—he always signs his name in full, with some flourish—is a traveling salesman. He sells industrial textile soaps, setting off by train every Monday morning with a suitcase of samples to extol to factory managers across England all the way through until Friday. He is away on that autumn day in 1929. So Veda must try to reach him wherever he is, perhaps in Leeds or Liverpool in a commercial hotel. They do not have a telephone, and neither do any of their neighbors, so she goes to the post office at the back of Stow's Stores to send that frantic telegram. Mrs. Stow offers comfort; Mr. Stow gathers other villagers to join in the search. I suspect they have private thoughts about where Betty is, and even who might have taken her. Perhaps that is why the police are not involved until the following day. But their guesses will all be wrong.

The hue and cry ran along the coast from one village to the next, from Chapel to Ingoldmells and Anderby Creek. If the missing child left any footprints in the sand, they led nowhere, or faded out too soon. If there were witnesses who could offer something more useful than the color of Betty's dress, then they never spoke up, even when the policeman called. The first day passed with no news of her, and then another, by which stage the police could surely offer only dwindling reassurance. Three more days of agony followed. And then Betty was discovered, unharmed and dressed in brand-new clothes—now red, as if through some curious Doppler shift—in a house not twelve miles from the shore.

My mother has no memory of these events. Nobody ever spoke of them at home, in Chapel St. Leonards or anywhere else. It was another half century and more before she even learned of the kidnap.

The dead may be invisible, but they are not absent; so writes Saint Augustine. We carry their influence, their attitudes, their genes. Their behavior may form or deform our own. The actions of all these villagers have affected my mother right up to this day, most particularly the behavior of her parents and those who took her. Her life began with a false start and continued with a long chain of deceptions, abetted by acts of communal silence so determined they have continued into my life too. The mystery of what happened, of how it changed her and her own children, has run through my days ever since I first heard of the incident on the beach thirty years ago. Then it seemed to me that all we needed was more evidence to solve it, more knowledge in the form of documents, letters, hard facts. But to my surprise, the truth turns out to pivot on images as much as words. To discover it has involved looking harder, looking closer, paying more attention to the smallest of visual details—the clues in a dress, the distinctive slant of a copperplate hand, the miniature faces in the family album.

I picture each scene, as we all do with puzzles, assembling the evidence in the mind's eye. But the habit is also involuntary. My mother is an artist, my father was an artist; it is the family profession. Every evening, after teaching at Edinburgh College of Art, my father would draw for hours in his sketchbook. These drawings took the form of lyrical abstractions of the golden mean, the cuneiform alphabet, the newly revealed wonders of the subatomic particle, occasionally a couple of high-wire acrobats for his children. But recollections of the day would materialize too: a student at an easel, a bowl of spaghetti cooked by my mother—all conceived within frames, just as her doodles during a phone call would appear as finished tableaux. She might even draw the telephone itself, with its spiraling cord, add an elaborate table, then set the table with dahlias, all while hanging on for a dentist's appointment. She taught me how to remember paintings in those long-ago days before I could take their images home from the museum in the blink of an iPhone: first draw the frame, then summarize the main shapes and volumes in rapid thumbnail. Rembrandt sketched a Titian in just the same way at an Amsterdam auction. Even the picturing of pictures is ingrained.

This is almost the only way that I can think, in fact. And I have thought of this day on Chapel Sands all these years, trying to imagine who took Betty—"presumed stolen" is the police phrase—and how it could have happened, to gauge the force of it, the effect on her and on everyone involved. I picture Veda, bewildered, afraid, inexperienced, not long in charge of this child who is suddenly lost, perhaps never in charge of her again on the sands; George, trying to control the situation at a distance, rushing home to take charge; Betty, an inkling in blue, moving about the beach in the last of the light, and then gone. The more I have discovered, the more I realize that there was a life before the kidnap, and a life afterwards, and they were never the same for anyone.

2

The House

The character of Lincolnshire as it meets the sea is level and low, a great plane of clay-plowed fields and bare-branched willows that spreads into the distance like a Dutch winter land-scape. Every modest haystack and spire seems a mile high as you pass beneath the wheeling arc of bright sky. In the north, the land is reclaimed from the sea; in the south, the fens give way to briny marshes. The flattest of all English counties, Lincolnshire is also the least altered by time, or mankind, and still appears nearly medieval in its ancient maze of dikes and paths. It faces the Netherlands across the water, and on a tranquil day it sometimes feels as if you could walk straight across to the rival flatness of Holland.

Chapel, at the time of the kidnap, was a hamlet of some three hundred souls, mostly living in red-brick farm cottages before the advent of electricity or cars, when paraffin lamps lit the dim windows at night and potatoes were still lugged to market on carts. A few dozen houses, three shops, a church dwarfed by a large vicarage: the whole community was arranged along a narrow strip between the brown farmland and the sandy shore. But Betty lived some way outside this huddle in the first of four terraced houses built in 1918 by an uncle (rich) and humbly rented by her grateful parents (poor) at what may have been a charitable rate, given George's modest salary. I have seen this terrace in old photographs, marooned in the outlying fields like a folly. Each house had an attic and a false balcony on the second floor, as if its occupants were likely to step out in evening dress to admire the view. Even the name, St. Leonard's Villas, feels too grandiose for such a rural spot, rather like its architect, Uncle Hugh, who had made his fortune during the Raj. But the interiors were much the same as every other two-up two-down of the time: a pair of cramped bedrooms, an outside privy, and a mothballed parlor too expensive to heat, working families living in the kitchen instead.

George and Veda were forty-nine years old when Betty entered their lives. Victorian children, Edwardian newlyweds, they had been married for more than two decades. As late as 1929, there was an antique atmosphere to their home, even though it was comparatively new. They shared one dark bedroom, into which an iron cot was now placed; the other, painted in mauve and black distemper, was occupied by Veda's elderly mother, Rebecca, otherwise known as Granny Crawford. She, at least, knew something about small children, having raised six of her own.

Into this gloom came a little blue-eyed child from the present, laughing and smiling and enlivening their days. I know her from the family album. My mother and I used to turn the pages together when I too was a child, marveling at the black-and-white lives condensed in these diminutive images. Betty cradles a stuffed rabbit, plays at laundry with a washboard and a cake of carbolic, beams back at her father, George. His camera works best outdoors, where the light is not so hard to control. So here she is bathing her doll by the outside privy, standing among spring tulips, trying out her new fairy bicycle in a photograph exactly as small as it appears on this page.

There is no obvious sorrow, at least not yet. Who could afford to photograph long faces on a salesman's salary? Betty at three always looks as buoyant as a skylark through the lens of George's Box Brownie. And there is so much for his new little child to play with: an aviary for songbirds in the garden, built by George; a ball attached to a length of elastic for her to bash with a bat; a miniature washing line for the doll's garments. Life is sunlit out there in the garden. The camera requires it, but so does George. My mother recalls his abrupt orders to turn to the light, pose this way or that, stand still, keep smiling, show her hands. "The photographer's tyranny," as she has written. The older she gets in these photographs, the more the effort to obey becomes visible in the strained fixity of her expression. I see what she remembers.

Because you have asked me, dear daughter, here are my earliest recollections. It is an English domestic genre canvas of the 20s and 30s, layered over with decades of fading and darkening, but your curiosity has begun to make all glow a little. And perhaps a few figures and events may turn out to be restored through the telling. Straightaway, however, there is a dilemma; for without invention I can say nothing about the first three years. They leave no imprint on my conscious memory.

For my twenty-first birthday, my mother gave me the gift I most wanted: the tale of her early life. This memoir is short, ending with her teenage years, but its writing carries so much of her grace, her truthful eloquence and witness, her artist's way of looking at the world. She was fifty-six when she sat down to write and still knew nothing about the kidnap, or her existence before it, except that she had been born in a mill house in 1926; or rather, as it seemed to her, that some other baby had arrived there. "I am Betty, she was Grace; she was not the real me." She imagines this stranger's advent in the summer's heat, "in a room probably made even hotter by the bread-baking, for milling and making went together in those days, and on the wall, huge shadows turning and returning as the mill sails glide round the huge Lincolnshire sky outside. But of course nothing of this seems ever to have happened, and instead I go back only to St. Leonard's Villas, and the one name and person I know, which is three-year-old Betty."

She and I used to make up stories to fill those empty years. Because she was fair, as am I, we imagined a Viking heritage, with visions of the open water between Lincolnshire and Norway. Unafraid of the sea, a fine swimmer, she must be a Scandinavian child who had somehow fetched up on an English shore. Or perhaps she had origins in Holland; didn't we love tulips, cheese, and Vermeer, whose silent girls, with their absorbing letters and their pearls, she gave me as postcard distractions during a bout of mumps at eight? This version became especially popular after our only trip abroad as a family, when a Dutch patron invited my father to Amsterdam. We saw the ingenious dikes and polders, just like their Lincolnshire equivalents; visited, and ate, Edam and Gouda; and returned home with golden-brown memories of Rembrandt in the Rijksmuseum. Rembrandt, who is said to have made the reverse journey to Lincolnshire in the 1650s, taking a quick ship across the North Sea to escape personal chaos, and make some money painting "sea-faring men's pictures." So says the antiquary George Vertue, and nobody has ever been able to disprove him.

The smiling child of the family album had a different life indoors. Until the age of five, she slept in her parents' crepuscular bedroom. "My first recollection: the dread hour of bedtime, the dark and sleepless solitude. Whole nights seemed to be spent restlessly awake, listening to their downstairs voices, and falling asleep only when they came up and I was safe. One night I vividly recall being held up to the window, seeing nothing but fearful blackness, while the house shook to the sound of a terrifying rumble. The word *earthquake* entered my language."

Betty was four when the Dogger Bank earthquake shook England, and chimneys, walls, and spires collapsed all across the county. But a stronger memory by far, from this age, is of an incident concerning her grandmother.

Granny Crawford is in floor length black frocks, a quiet pale face beneath white hair with severe centre parting coiled at the back. Very deaf, frail, and alarmingly given to nose-bleeds, she was a great irritation to my father. One day during a meal, he shouted angrily at her for incorrectly holding her knife and fork. I had never before witnessed such ill-temper, so unjust; and I can feel now the moment of stunned terror between grandmother, mother and I, as this abuse shook the very plates it seemed; and little grandmother sat stock still, looking down with folded hands. In subsequent years I was to hear the same anger often directed against mother and myself, and I must truthfully say that I never forgave him any of it. Probably because of that first time, when straight away I saw the indefensible docility of the old lady attacked on so trivial a matter by his great sledgehammer of rage, I began to turn resentfully silent—this being the only weapon I could muster. Fortunately it was the acceptable characteristic: little children should be seen and not heard being THE great maxim.

Granny Crawford died at the age of eighty-five, just after Betty's fifth birthday. Veda dreamed that her mother was moving around the bedroom in an upright coffin, gently reassuring everyone that she was happy. This transfiguration was a gift to poor bereaved

Veda, the vacated room Betty's inheritance. But it was full of the ghost of the departed. She became newly fearful.

> Sometimes a night-light burned in a saucer beside my bed, but I spent anxious hours watching in case it went out, and of course the matches were not in my care. A later treasure was my first bed-side lamp, made by George, with an opaque glass globe hand-painted with a bright spray of forget-me-nots. It delighted me with the sophistication of its on-off button and I think gave a very dim light, not enough to read by; and in any case one did not dare overstrain the battery, for then would come a night of total darkness.

My mother once read the birthday memoir to my twelve-year-old twin daughters, who were incredulous that she could not sleep for watching the light, or use the lamp in case it drained the battery. Living in a London that is never dark, they have no idea of night's obliterating blackness in the middle of nowhere in the days before electricity; and, mercifully, no experience of a home in which you could not call for help. My mother sweetly laughed, but I wonder if she really found this funny or simply treasured their innocence.

The one happy night was Christmas Eve, when Betty was allowed to stay up to fill the pastry cases with dark, spicy mincemeat. Then it was upstairs for the ceremony of pinning up a pillowcase.

This brought the sleep-defying turbulence felt by all children trying so hard to give Father Christmas the conditions he seems to require: he won't come unless you go to sleep. At last, opening one's eyes to Christmas Day, looking unbelievably to see that it has magically happened, and bulky shapes are pushing out last night's empty bag. Strangely enough I cannot summon up what those things were, except for the sublime and the ridiculous—a pink sugar mouse and a Bible. This latter, brown leather, was pronounced over solemnly by my father: "This is the greatest gift you will ever receive." I felt the gravity stopping my breath. But the greatest gift was a terrible disappointment, with its hundreds of very thin pages, its thousands of baffling words in the tiniest print, incomprehensible except for a few well loved stories, so that I looked only at the pictures—sepia photographs of the Holy Land, disappointingly stony and bare, with the occasional glum shepherd. It was my least favourite book.

On Christmas Day there were never any other family or children, only two elderly friends.

Kate and Tom Stevenson were (I think) a married couple, though they could have been brother and sister, so alike in shortness, stoutness, redness of face and hugeness of appetite. Tom always fell asleep in the afternoon, cigarette in mouth and the ash dropping on to his waistcoat. One had to be subdued for hours in deference to the grown-up needs for digestive recovery, and then later in the evening out would come the carving knife again and everyone would say how much nicer turkey was cold. This went on year after year, Tom's white walrus moustache growing more nicotined as he became more adept at smoking whole cigarettes without once holding them in his hands. He suffered dreadful coughs and breathlessness and at last came a Christmas without him any more. He left his fascinating pocket-barometer to my mother. Kate once gave me a whole pound-note for neatly cutting the grass on his grave.

The barometer sits before me now, a sturdy brass prophet for the hand, able to predict the future simply by configuring wind direction, season, and barometric pressure. Its fragile needle runs from miserable to fair, although for Betty it always seemed to be blowing and dull. In curlicues on the white dial is the name of its maker, J. Newton, cousin to the great physicist Sir Isaac, whose gravity-confirming apple fell in a Lincolnshire orchard not twenty miles from St. Leonard's Villas, though Betty never heard anything about him. This circular relic lies in a saucer that also came from Chapel, last of a Willow pattern service permanently shelved in the parlor. Once, and only once, Betty persuaded Veda to serve Christmas dinner on these dishes with their blue-and-white pictures. "We took them all very carefully down and washed off the dust of ages, and she felt scandalised to be committing this sacrilege, though giving way to my pronouncement that such lovely things were meant to be used."

Veda never played with Betty. It is an abiding sadness in the memoir, which my mother explains to herself as the result of all the oppressive housework required before electricity and hot water. She remembers much beating of carpets and shoveling of ashes, the salting of mutton to keep it from rotting, the soaking of cucumber slices in dishes of vinegar to make them marginally more luxurious. Perhaps Veda was worn out by her chores, but I wonder if she was also unaccustomed to small children, shy, uncertain, possibly undermined by the kidnap. She had some help in the person of a tiny villager named Lizzie Cornell, who came every Thursday to thump the clothes and turn the mangle. "I see her now up to the elbows in a huge tub of suds, going in and out to the washing line with a mouthful of wooden pegs. She was Veda's great companion and our chief recording angel, bearer of village news." A black-clad widow of several decades, Lizzie was not very much younger than Granny Crawford, whose husband had died, leaving her with those six small children, before she was forty. Both of these wise women, bitterly experienced, must surely have known something about Betty's past before St. Leonard's Villas.

Chapel news seemed outlandish and rare because Betty never went there. Around the age of five, she started to become aware of the oppressive confines of her existence. She was not allowed to play with village children, or to travel the half mile to that mecca of forbidden shops. She was only allowed to go to church with Veda, or to the beach with George, who was morose on the sands, denouncing the winds in winter and the feckless sun-seekers in summer. Other than the Stevensons at Christmas and Lizzie on Thursdays, there were no visitors to the house. Betty must stay inside the garden, behind a hedge as high (in my mind) as the forest in "Rapunzel," or remain glumly indoors with Veda. Naturally, with hindsight, this must have had something to do with the kidnap; and it may be that Betty had been too young to notice the extreme protectiveness before. But for her it was a cruel imprisonment, and her jailer was the fiercely strict and possessive George. In all the childhood tales that she told, I scarcely heard his name once. He left no letters, diaries, or documents through which he could speak for himself, and my mother mainly seemed to mourn the disappearance of a toy theater and a miniature house he made for her that held better memories of those days when they still knew one another. I had no idea that he fought in the Boer War and was a medaled veteran and a draftsman of distinction, receiving an award during his time in the army—a possible career that was mysteriously derailed. I only knew that George was angry, bronchitic, dictatorial, and that he was a liar.

Once, my mother took me out of school to see the paintings of Édouard Vuillard, then on show in Edinburgh. We were enthralled by this master of the muffled interior, of unspoken emotions in Parisian apartments, particularly his scenes of the lamplit flat in rue Truffaut where Vuillard lived and worked with his seamstress mother for sixty years, hemmed in among the cushions, patterned walls, and bales of billowing cloth. One painting instantly stirred memories of her own childhood. It is *Interior: Mother and Sister of the Artist*. There is the characteristic sense of time arrested and the world excluded in Vuillard's art, of life reduced to an airless room. The old woman sits like Picasso's Gertrude Stein, hands to splayed knees and quite composed. She at least has some independence. But the girl seems to be tangled in the wallpaper unnoticed, a pale specter struggling to free herself from—or is it to hide within?—its camouflage. Even the picture appears to be trapping her: she has to bow her head to fit inside the frame.

This was how it felt to my mother, indoors with Veda among the dark oak furniture and the stifling atmosphere. As the years passed, and George became increasingly tense and bad-tempered, his Friday-night return from work only tightened the ratchet. The curtains in their house were always drawn before dusk. The walls of domesticity closed in.

There were no pictures in Betty's house. Writers nearly always seem to have at least one book, but artists so often come from bare walls, from an imageless home where paintings are seen for the first time only in churches or galleries. It is the commonest thing to have grown up with no art at all and still become an artist, as happened to both my mother and my father. After all, sight has primacy; the whole visible world is contained in our eyes.

Instead she pored over the half-inch snapshots of the Holy Land printed on the stamps for her Sunday school attendance book and gazed at the blue bridges crossed by fleeing Chinese lovers on the Willow pattern plates. She wondered at the scarlet thistles, so unnatural, on the packet of Isdale's eponymous carbolic soap, and at the label on the Camp Coffee and Chickory Essence bottle that shows a Gordon Highlander being served a cup of this ersatz stuff by a Sikh soldier who has the very same bottle on his tray, so that the picture within a picture could in theory go on forever.

When we went to Amsterdam, we were both amazed to see the shops and houses densely tiled with blue-and-white images of the world in every degree from the widest landscape to the smallest daisy, from the windmill to the fiddler, the ice skate, and the butter pat. My mother rejoiced in this: no Dutch child could have grown up without these modest wall-to-wall depictions.

Pictures hold thoughts, ideas, and memories like the pockets of a coat. Our sense of other people's lives, as they describe them or we read about them, often coalesce in the mind's eye this way. So when I think of Chapel St. Leonards in the 1930s, and the Elstons' lives there, it is partly through my mother's words but also through the work of an English artist of that period, Eric Ravilious. I picture the kettle singing on its hearth at Number 1 exactly like this:

Heavy to lift, its handle too hot to hold except wrapped in a cloth, the great vessel builds to its projectile steam. Ravilious moves it to the side of the flames; otherwise it might whistle all day. This will do perfectly for Veda's kitchen, this emblematic object, ready for washing-up water and steady cups of tea. *Put the kettle on*: the unspoken caption. And when it's taken off, thick encrustations of soot will have to be scraped from its sides and the iron polished all over again, another of her Sisyphean duties.

The kettle comes from Ravilious's graphic alphabet, designed for Wedgwood in 1936, when my mother was ten. It is a fantastical lexicon, from the eerie *D* for diver down among the fishes to the *N* for a new moon bright as an eye at midnight. These tiny images ran around the mugs from which my brother and I drank tea as children decades later, and they still spell out Chapel to me. Here is the

flatfish with its glinting scales, caught on Chapel beach; the eggs, snug in their Lincolnshire nest. Here is a geranium leaf from the pots in Veda's garden, and flowers picked from the hedgerows for her spotted jug. The box of matches is half-open, revealing its blue-tipped contents, an object shaking its familiar music in George's pocket as he walks home with a cigarette on Fridays. A quince dangles from a branch, ready to be plucked for Lizzie Cornell's jelly. *Y* and *Z*, separated by a brief sand-colored strip, show a yacht on the sea at Chapel and the German zeppelin my mother saw above the church steeple one night: "a huge dark shape, no wings or propellers, just as a slow looming body as unbelievable as if the moon itself had descended."

The alphabet could also be seen as a self-portrait. It shows what Ravilious loved: the secret door in the kitchen-garden wall, the scrubbed table bearing a fresh new loaf for tea, the rolling Wiltshire hills with pictures of horses cut into the chalk. It looks at first like the enchanted world of childhood. But there is an enigmatic singularity to every image. His pictures ask you to pay attention to ordinary beauty, to look at the overlooked once more, and they chime with our folk knowledge of blue-and-white china, cold linoleum, the hoed rows of vegetable gardens, the beach hut, and the twisting weather vane: Chapel St. Leonards, for me.

My mother first saw the works of Ravilious when she got away to college and passed though the looking glass into the land of art. She has exactly his attentiveness. And we have looked at his work so often together and found in it the picture of our lives. In Edinburgh, where I grew up, we would go to the botanical gardens every Sunday, loving the regimental drills of pansies that came up bright even in winter, peering into the glasshouses where the gardeners raised the new plants. Ravilious's *Greenhouse* revives the recollections every time, and seems to carry in itself the atmosphere of memory. Everything is in perfect order, and yet there is no sign of a gardener, unless perhaps divine? Door opens onto door onto door. The perspective is pristine, the painting so clear, light, and symmetrical in both form and content, the white paper burning through the foliage like sunshine. It is the greenhouse from paradise.

Ravilious has been criticized for the joyousness of his art, as if he ought to find more anguish in life, especially with the approach of the Second World War. But there is mystery in that joy, a kind of surprise that the plain, scrubbed world could be quite so beautiful. When the war came, he served as both pilot and official war artist, posted to missions off the coast of Iceland. In his Arctic watercolors, magnificent white light ricochets across shivering waters beneath a sky streaked with silvery vapor trails and planes. On an autumn day in 1942, he himself went up in one of those aircraft and vanished, his fate another disappearance at sea. He was not yet forty; the lost genius of British art.

When Betty finally reached school age, George could contain his growing daughter no longer. But he sent her only as far as the house next door, to a little dame school run by a neighbor. There were ten pupils at Miss Turney's establishment, most of them arriving through fields and lanes from outlying farms on bicycles. Whereas Betty merely went down one front path and up the next into an identical parlor on the other side of the wall.

"At Miss Turney's we sat jammed up all day in small desks poring over exercises with pens and ink, the sort of treatment that would be considered practically mental cruelty to infants these days. One afternoon the whole school was kept in detention while she waited for somebody to admit to drawing on the wall. Nobody said anything and minute after minute passed, until eventually the silent tension produced a false confession from me, simply so that I could escape the cramped classroom." Excoriated by Miss Turney, Betty was punished all over again at home, quite unjustly, for telling lies. Only much later did it dawn upon her that she really had been the culprit after all, inadvertently scraping the wall, pen in hand, as she raised the lid of her desk in that narrow parlor.

The roots of claustrophobia began to grow.

Among the other pupils next door were the two daughters of Bert Parrish, who ran a dairy on the other side of the road. George photographed Mary and Esther with Betty in the garden, all three got up in St. Trinian's gymslips and panama hats. She would never forget these girls, the first friends she was ever allowed to have, tolerated for playing school or hospital as long as they stayed clearly in Veda's sight and did not try to entice her across the road. Their image is almost invisible now: two gangly girls of seven and nine in a couple of inches of blanched sepia. Their shadows linger, just, but the real girls were gone in a moment. One afternoon they came round asking for Betty and were told that she wouldn't be playing with them that day, or ever again. She was forbidden to speak to them in the street or even in the parlor at Miss Turney's. When another pupil, a cheerful little lad called Murray, came looking for her on his bike, Betty was only allowed to communicate with him through the tangled thicket of hedge.

The Parrish photograph appears in the family album with a note about their friendship in my mother's adult hand. Without her inscriptions, I would have no idea that the villagers sitting at a long table in a hazy orchard, like a summer gathering out of Chekhov, include the young George and Veda Elston in 1914. No idea that the apron Veda is wearing in 1935 was cross-stitched by nine-year-old Betty; that the new bicycle she is receiving for that year's birthday is a gift from George, suspiciously given around the time that Mary and Esther were banned with the promise of limited trips down the lane. She puts names to faces wherever she can, fishing people from the sea of oblivion, and even trying to identify the most baffling situations, as when four people are gathered ceremonially around a piece of driftwood on the shore. But there is one image that has no caption or comment, no date or explanation, and that is the one tucked inside the back cover of the album. I have sometimes wondered if it was meant to be hidden there.

It shows George holding a child on the ridge at Chapel Sands. She can only be a couple of years old, dressed in what looks like a knitted frock with matching bloomers, and her feet are probably bare, though they are not in the image. Nor are his, for his legs are tucked beneath him and he is trying hard to hold her close and still for the lens. She isn't moving, although there is a slight blur about her face.

Scene, pose, relationship: all are uncomfortable. His right hand clasps her tight; his left hand pinions hers on his leg. Her fingernails are a trio of white dots. She is not paying attention to the camera, not looking at the photographer or relating to the man in whose grip she is held. You might say she looks depressed.

George is in his Sunday best: good blazer, light trousers, silk bow tie. What color? Not black, like his double-breasted blazer, perhaps dark crimson or navy. His panama hat lies carefully placed on the sand beside him. Its ribbon matches the blazer.

Behind them a fraction of sea is visible. Before them is the photographer. Together they make a trio.

But what kind of trio, and who is in charge? It may be that the child wants to wriggle away from the man, return to the photographer, or be free of them both to head off and play on the sands. She wants to be out of the picture.

This photograph shows George with Grace. Her name is written on the back in another hand. She is not called Betty, and she has not yet come to live with the Elstons, an event that is still in the future. So how can they already have met, how can Grace be appearing with George now, and who is taking the shot? I have never yet known the strange circumstances in which this photograph came to be taken, and neither has my mother.

3

The Village

Number 1 was generally held to be the best of St. Leonard's Villas because of the enclosed garden that ran down one side. "Its chief glory," recalled my mother, "was a sycamore from whose massy branches hung a swing. This was at once a delight and a grief to me, for I loved the glimpses it gave of life over the top of the hedge, then hated their sudden loss."

My mother's first proper painting was of this sycamore. It deserves this pole position in her fledgling career because everything that could be seen from the swing's zenith became precious entertainment, and without that tree I too would have little sense of the world outside her home. She would watch Old Cade the farmer prodding two cows to pasture, his slow to-and-fro the measure of each country day; and trailing his sheep in the opposite direction a gaunt shepherd with a long white beard who looked like George Bernard Shaw. Occasionally she might spot Miss Button, in jodhpurs and long woolen socks, flat cap concealing her hair, riding by on a gigantic tricycle. Or Mr. Short the gardener passing towards church in his melancholy capacity as bell-ringer for funerals, tolling the age of the deceased out across the fields around Chapel.

The dairyman Bert Parrish, father of Esther and Mary, never walked an inch if he could ride his bicycle instead, driving his cows along with a defunct stub of cigarette between his lips.

It was the general opinion that he was the laziest dairyman in the world, and how he ever made a living from the gallon or two of milk that resulted from his tired daily labours nobody knew. Esther and Mary went round neighbouring back doors with a milk-can and two ladles, pint and half-pint, to fill jugs and collect a few pence; while Mrs. Parrish managed the dark and dubious dairy, not a cool white-washed chamber with bowls of cream and frothing sweet milk but somewhere one did not peer into closely. Bert spared the cows any inconvenience of hygiene; scrubbing and sterilising were too demanding of energy. Any time I caught a glimpse of either Bert or his wife indoors, they were at repose in a dim kitchen shiftlessly enjoying the ticking of the grandfather clock, spread slackly about on dilapidated armchairs. I have never liked milk ever since.

As a child, Betty wondered if the Parrish girls were banned because of the state of their parents' dairy. As a teenager, she thought it might be more to do with class, and a village pecking order so refined that a traveling salesman like George, no matter how unsuccessful, was a man of the world who rode trains compared to a herder of cattle. Later still, it dawned on her that the Parrishes must have presented some kind of threat to the Elstons, sufficient that they had to be blocked. It remained as baffling as the apartheid that put one end of Chapel and all its children out of bounds, or a strange shunning of the Elstons themselves. St. Leonard's Villas received its daily bread each morning by van. Betty would watch from the window as Harold Blanchard, the baker's son, arrived with a large basket on his arm. He never looked back, and he never came up their path, delivering loaves to every other house in the terrace except Number 1.

That I did not know the occupants of the other houses is some proof of the narrowness of life up until then, but even my all-powerful father could not put a wall around me forever. The fact is that I was ageing and must be allowed outside his sole

jurisdiction. Veda began to take me down the lane on duty vis-
its to Old Cade and his sister Mrs. Butler. Cade was slowly
dying, raked by bronchitic spasms which he ended with success
by spitting into an empty Golden Syrup tin. He was deaf and
gruff, his eyes like a weepy bloodhound, bony old hands clasped
over a walking stick. Mrs. Butler was no more alluring, black
dressed and stuffed looking, with a few gray hairs skimped
back to a bun no bigger than a marble—not a tooth left in her
head and a mouth consequently sunk into a tiny round pucker,
which made it impossible to understand a word she lisped.

Veda's other duties seemed no less alarming. She was a church-
goer, unlike George, and took her daughter the reluctant mile to St.

Leonard's Church each Saturday to do the brasses and flowers. "I would carry the bag of stiff gray polishing rags and—well away from me—a bunch of daffodils with oozing stuck stems, or rank smelling marguerites alive with creeping black insects. She would lift the heavy vases and crucifix from the altar into the vestry, where we buffed the dull green film from the brass. I used to nose about in the musty cupboards, where the old vicar kept a chamber pot, and some vinegary communion wine, feeling death-shadowed."

I have been to that church, found Veda's name in the old parish records, sat where she sat every Sunday beneath the high windows through which the sun's rays angle down, making fireflies out of the dust motes. In the green grass outside are the headstones of Old Cade and his sister, and so many of the people in this story. Veda used to tend the village graves, replenishing the family flowers, while Betty drained the fetid water from the jam jars. The smell of decay horrified her and she longed to dance home, light-footed, to her doll; a child too much surrounded by age and death.

Memories calcify over the years; everything grows more extreme—the brightness incandescent, the darkness infinitely worse. For my daughters, the birthday memoir is overwhelmingly concerned with hardship, isolation, and horror. Everything is frightening or forbidden. But my sense is that this was my mother's reality. She did not live with merry or demonstrative people; her parents were fearful of something unknown, something that was never mentioned or explained but would one day cause a crisis in that very church. Their dread passed straight to her.

At school, the teachers put her forward for a local production of *A Midsummer Night's Dream*, with Betty as a fairy in gauzy green wings. A report in the local paper commends her performance and announces that Betty Elston, aged nine and already excelling in English, is the winner of a county-wide essay competition. Veda took her to collect the medal, and afterwards to tea at the Vine Hotel, where Veda's father had once been the innkeeper and she herself had grown up. In those days it was still a couthy establishment, serving the Midlands gentry who came for the fresh air and sea views available from the higher-priced rooms. George took his drinks at the Vine, and my mother once had a seasonal job there as a waitress. Every year, as Chapel metamorphosed from winter silence to summer noise, heat baked the beach and the Vine filled up with customers. The Elstons sometimes crammed in paying guests too, to make ends meet, Veda cooking hot dinners and mangling extra sheets through July and August. A box sat by the door for strangers to shake the sand from their feet.

Once, somewhere, I glimpsed George's order book before it disappeared from our home and recollection. Perhaps it was thick with sales; or perhaps not, for there never seems to have been any money. How he paid for the little dame school is an abiding enigma. There was the letting of rooms and the sporadic selling of vegetables; and Veda's scrimping was an art in itself. But George surfaces in local newspapers trying to sell a crystal wireless, a chair, and even his old overcoat.

I can imagine more, of course, from their early life together: the long childless decades, Veda's loneliness as George departs each Monday (or is it relief, given his temper?), the tending of those vegetables and the cleaning of those paraffin lamps. And all of this went on for years and shadowy years before my mother arrived. Whereupon everything passes into living color, for she remembers, and writes it all down for me.

Chapel had a tribal population, the recurring families extensive and intermarried. My mother loved to rhyme their Lincolnshire names:

Hipkin and Harness, Capron and Stow
Pimperton, Balding, Budabent, Crow.
Ailsby and Lenton, Raynor and Kirk,
Button and Boddice, Meadows and Sirk.

Mrs. Ailsby was a gentle, sweet-faced woman with a teenage daughter called Annie. Her name sounded to me like an apple and to paint her would be to paint a truly apple-cheeked girl, fair curly hair and awesomely old at fourteen. One morning she was clearly upset and whispering to her equally grown-up friend. Her mother had drowned in the dyke outside their house, which also flowed widely past my own. It had happened the night before, but poor Annie was still sent off to school.

Some months later, the jovial butcher Mr. Lenton was suddenly spoken about by Lizzie Cornell in hushed not-in-front-of-the-children tones. "Some dread thing called pneumonia had struck him down. I could hardly imagine it—out one afternoon delivering meat; 48 hours later, dead."

Lizzie, who had an exact recall for every one of the Chapel marriages and their outcomes, was friends with the gravedigger who had to bury these poor souls. His name, unbelievably, was Arthur Graves. He and his wife, Polly, lived in a cottage on that short sandy path between Betty's house and the beach, so she encountered them many times. "Naturally their name was enough to make them fearful. They were always worried and ashen, two gate-leaners watching the world. Looking back, I think what life had they? He earning a pittance for his sad work, she never out of her long apron with scrubbing brush or hard at it in the cabbage patch of a garden.

I suppose I had no awareness of the beauty of her cottage-garden flowers in those days, only the sense of anxiety."

On the beach, occasionally, were some sinister figures called the Caprons, who lived beyond the village precincts and were more than once referred to in the press. "Their voices come back to me; they spoke 'posh,' she in particular, very high and rapid. They were regarded with suspicion, reputedly (hushed whispering) spies for the Germans in the First World War, sending lantern signals from the coast out to sea." They seem archetypes straight out of Miss Marple, and are mentioned in connection with the *Hindenburg*. When that dark zeppelin crossed the coastline at Chapel in 1936, people at the Vine were able to read the tiny German words on the side of the massive gray balloon. One witness said that it loomed larger than the whole of Chapel; another that the figures looking down from the windows were clearly spies. Were the Caprons signaling up from the beach?

Veda and George wanted Betty to play the piano. Not having one of their own, they took her to practice on the old upright belonging to a church friend and neighbor called Mrs. Simpson. The idea was that Betty should keep the music in her head, returning home to repeat whatever she had just played on a paper keyboard drawn by George. The minor keys were blacked in with graphite; he made a cardboard chessboard the same way that survived into my own childhood. I have the stub of pencil I believe he might have used. Our house in Edinburgh was full of pencils, sharpened to perfection by my father. But this one was not Faber or Staedtler or any brand name I had ever heard of, and was of a finer bore altogether: a thin wooden tube, carved with a blade and narrowing to a long bayonet of black lead. A century old, and so worn down with work there is scarcely an inch of it left.

If only there were photographs of George's other indoor creations, legendary to me through my mother's telling: the miniature replica he made of their own home, complete with one-inch balconies and cutlery soldered out of hairpins. The toy theater with changeable scenery and gliding velvet curtains that he fitted with footlights in four different colors: white for daylight, yellow for gaslight, green for storms, red for sunset and the Great Fire of London. In the birthday memoir, she eulogizes these wondrous creations with a gratitude I find intensely moving, remembering every good thing that she can, a measure of her grace. For this generosity towards her very soon ceased, and she doesn't quite understand why it was shown in the first place. "Perhaps it is possible George made so much of me when I was very young because he had no other family." Might it not have been because he loved her?

Nobody ever used that word in their house. This is easy to imagine from the clipped speech of English films in that "low, dishonest decade," as W. H. Auden called the 1930s. My mother remembers the laconic briskness of household communications: Fetch the coal, sit up straight, close the curtains, for heaven's sake oil your machine (George's name, ever the engineer, for his daughter's bicycle). Off to work then, back on Friday. Best wishes written in block caps on her birthday card. Veda spoke in very short phrases, when she did speak. Keep yourself to yourself: George's terse refrain. Nobody was expansive, nobody ventured much into dialogue.

My mother, when she met my Scottish father, felt the immense relief of his talking. He was conversational with all, zany in his humor, precise in his eloquence. Tongue-tied even then, she could at last stop worrying about what to say because he would now do the job. She did not really learn to speak, she once confided, until she was nearly forty.

My own childhood memories tell the opposite: that she always had the words, that she could talk to anyone. I distinctly remember sitting on her knee at the age of two or three, down from bed, unable to sleep during one of my parents' parties. She is wearing a dress of sky-blue wool, white stockings, and green shoes. Round her neck is a long silver necklace set with turquoises that one of her friends has sent from Tehran. I am aware, somehow, of the elegance of these slender knees—elegant still, in old age—and the aura of Chanel No. 5, which my father has saved up to buy her. She still treasures this bottle, fifty years later, with its dying scent of what we imagined to be Paris in the 1930s. I am jingling the fragile bells on this necklace, and she is somehow managing to talk over the top of my head, and this noise, to half a dozen artists laughing in a blue haze of postprandial smoke. She will be giving everything she has to this double act, comforting me while putting them at their ease, always torn between home and the outside world.

My mother, on the other hand, has no memories from her first three years, only a vague impression of warm strawberry jam. I used to find this astonishing: How could she have no recall of life's opening gambit? Teenagers, with so little living to remember, are especially impatient of such adult lapses. But when I look back on my own beginnings, I have only a few entirely independent memories: of being in my pram as it was knocked over, watching the sky wheeling over and landing in the soft brown soil of a flower bed that ran along the side of our Edinburgh house; no pain, only the thrill of seeing the world turned upside down. Of the day my brother cut his foot on a cigar tin someone had dropped in a paddling pool: the gashing gold metal, blood blossoming through the shallow water, the long retiring silence before his scream. He and I shared a bedroom with wallpaper of dolls from around the world— an Eskimo, a Cossack, an American Indian, with a disappointing juncture when the pattern repeated, as if there were no more nationalities—but perhaps his recollections help confirm it. Everything else is surely sustained by anecdote, family lore, the evidence of documents and snapshots. And perhaps experience develops into memory like a photograph: its latent imprint invisible to us until gradually fixed by conversation.

One childhood theory argues that our early recollections are entirely constructed through speech. We don't really remember events, only what is said about them. Everything that happens exists only in the remotest subconscious. This does not take account of the pictures streaming back and forth through our heads, suddenly slowing, momentarily fixed, or surfacing again through our dreams. But certainly Betty had nobody to reminisce with about her first three years, nobody to recount the events of the day, to answer questions, to establish or repeat anything. Nobody in her house had seen Grace's first steps or heard her first words; there were no pictures of picnics, paddling pools, or birthday parties, and no explanation of why this should be. If Betty ever asked any questions, no answers were given. There was just a baffling white gap.

To accompany the birthday memoir, my mother drew portraits of the people she saw. They are tiny vignettes, little figures surrounded by space as if briefly glimpsed or just returning from memory. Some are in pencil, others watercolor. Bert Parrish came onto the page very readily: "I found each detail of his appearance returning quite

clearly as I worked: the flat cap, greasy topped from pressing against the cows' flanks at milking time; dirty flannel shirt worn collarless and with flapping cuffs undone; black waistcoat; no buttons; the perpetual cigarette stub in the greenish-pale face, the smoke forever drifting up into narrowed eyes."

Polly Graves had to be in black and white: "The contrast between that white face and the worried eyebrows over the small black eyes, the dull hair scraped across a rather high forehead, kirby-gripped without a thought of appearance: it all became clear to my inner eye, She was so resurrected in my thoughts it hardly mattered that fifty years had passed, everything came back, even the hunched shoulders and the high querulous voice always delivering bad news."

These little sketches are archetypal, emblematic. They are not based on photographs; my mother had none to support, or to falsify, her memories. Even now, these people live in her mind's eye. Her childhood always had the character of myth or fable to me; the butcher, the baker, the bell-ringer and gravedigger: these were the legends of Chapel St. Leonards. When I recently came across a book of period photographs, compiled by a local historian, I was amazed to find that these people were actually real, and amazed again by my mother's accuracy. My favorite was the village draper, so tall, thin, and pale. Her name was Lily Boddice, significant of both her white face and the undergarments she sold. She was to be seen, invariably, with her hands flexed upon the counter in an attitude of tense rebuttal.

Lily Boddice's little shop was uninviting, colourless as herself. She was always "in the back"—some sort of kitchen, making onion-smelling dinners, and would come hurrying through when the shop bell signalled a customer. Her brownish-grey hair was in looped curtain shapes over her face, finishing up as coiled and plaited earphones. Her sallow skin, blank eyes and small unmoving mouth are perfectly clear in my memory. There she would stand, waiting for me to make some request. I was precocious about wool as a child and yet embarrassed to ask this unresponsive woman for some way-out new kind of yarn, poodle being one such novelty. The answer was always No.

These drawings are true to the memory of my mother's youth in Chapel, which she escaped as soon as she could. Looking at them now, I see that they are drawings of villagers as viewed by a child— people seen, but not yet understood. I found a school photograph of Lily Boddice from 1922 that does show an anxious, white-faced teenager towering above the other pupils. The photographic face seemed to come as living corroboration of the portrait. But Lily is not her face, nor her appearance, any more than the rest of us. When the Second World War came to Chapel, it brought service-men to the Lincolnshire coast. Lily met one of them and quite suddenly gave up the miserable drapery for married happiness. There is the split-second image; and there is the reality of the whole long life.

Lily Boddice, Bert Parrish, Polly Graves—they all knew about the kidnap, knew far more about Betty's story than she did. So did Mrs. Simpson, who owned the piano, and whom I would meet fifty years later in a journey back to Chapel to try to find out about my mother's past. Everything that happened to her depended on the complicity of these villagers, upon their willingness to keep silent for decades, in some cases right up until death. Neither Mrs. Simpson nor anybody else would tell us a thing. Even though George and Veda and almost everyone involved had long since died, and Mrs. Simpson had more knowledge than practically anybody else, she insisted on keeping their secrets.

4

The Baker's Daughter

There was a story my mother and I read together many times when I was a child. She even painted a watercolor, years later, to commemorate our mutual fascination. It came from an anthology called *The Golden Land*, which seemed to us a perfect description of the paradise in which it was set, for although the tale had a severe moral, it took place in a seductive America of sunny sidewalks, soda fountains, and towering pineapple sundaes.

This story told of a small-town baker somewhere out in the Midwest who was famous for his glazed crullers, whatever they might be, but principally for the spectacular artistry of his birthday cakes. Apricot with sugar doves, pistachio with lemon twirls, chocolate with cream and rose layers: these exotic objects glowed in my imagination far away in cold Edinburgh. I never wanted to eat them, only to see them; and eventually I did, not in a bakery but in a museum of modern art, through the works of the American painter Wayne Thiebaud. His radiant cakes with their gleaming cherries and luminous icing, the paint as rich as cream, speak of past joys and the happiness to come in simply looking at ordinary objects, in this case the circular perfection of cakes. These were proper fifties cakes too, just like the ones in the story, presented on stands in shop windows and in chiller cabinets lit with a misty blue air of nostalgia, as if these confections were already passing out of this world.

The baker in the story had a beautiful blond daughter who wore flouncy dresses, gold bracelets, and a ring with real gemstones. She would stroll proudly up and down the sidewalk sucking her beads

while all the other girls sighed with envy. The next best thing to being this princess, they thought, would surely be to walk up and down with her, burnished in reflected glory.

One child eventually achieves this dubious promotion. She is called Carmelita Miggs and she owns a pair of bronze shoes, which may be one reason why the baker's daughter condescends to be seen with her, and even to attend her birthday party. The baker promises to make a special cake for the occasion; but his daughter has her eye on the one in the window, a magnificent creation, famous all over town, which he always refuses to sell. While he is downstairs putting the finishing touches on a less distinguished effort, she steals this trophy and takes it to Carmelita's party, where everyone is duly overwhelmed. The party games over, the ice cream eaten, it is finally time for the cake. But the birthday girl cannot get her knife through the stiff icing, and neither can her mortified mother. They push harder and harder until suddenly the cake overturns—and is revealed to be nothing but an iced cardboard shell. The baker's daughter retreats in shame at what has proved to be no more than window dressing. Carmelita's party is over.

My mother's watercolor shows the difference between our two interpretations of "The Baker's Daughter." For me, this is a tale of foolish hopes and false promise; the golden girl is not what she seems, any more than the cake or the supposed friendship. I felt this most keenly in miserabilist adolescence, when the cardboard cake represented relationships and boys and quite probably life itself. I would have illustrated the story with the revelation of the sham cake—the drama of its hollow interior. But for my mother, the story centers entirely on Carmelita Miggs and all the other girls who want to be the baker's daughter, and crowd around her in the painting. The cake (although enviable too) is a complete irrelevance. This is a tale of yearning.

The birthday memoir brims with yearning. My mother longs to escape the house, the garden, the village of Chapel St. Leonards. She longs for the slightest hill in the long flat roads of her bicycling youth, or for the chance to catch a two-carriage train from the tiny local station, even just one stop to the next. At the age of ten, she still hasn't traveled farther than the seven miles to Skegness. Allowed to go there once to visit a schoolmate named Anne Scupholm whose parents were veritable potato magnates, in Lincolnshire terms, she was amazed by the dining table, the soup tureen, the enamel bath in its own special room. When they went to the beach, Anne wore coral-colored bathing shoes to protect her dainty feet (from what, I grimly wonder, for Skegness beach is all sand). My mother longed for such footwear.

Anne Scupholm is a name as familiar to me as Carmelita Miggs from childhood onwards; Anne and her wretched rubber sandals. I am immune to their charm, inoculated by defensiveness on my mother's behalf, but also, perhaps, by a kind of sad dismay that she still remembers those shoes.

Was her longing inevitable, the natural consequence of making do and shutting up, of confinement at home, dreams of escape, and the Elstons' necessarily frugal ethic? Or was it in some sense innate, her very own trait? I prefer to think it was circumstantial, and aggravated moreover by the only relatives she seemed to have known as a child, a family known to everybody in Chapel, in fact: the upper-crust Greens.

Captain Hugh Green was the uncle who let Number 1 St. Leonard's Villas to George. Mrs. Green was Veda's sister Hilda, younger by almost a decade. Their own vast house stood on the raised bank by the sea's edge. It had a colonial veranda, tiled hall, library, and billiards room, as well as the village's only private telephone and generator. This was the mansion from the Cluedo floor plan to me, and the Greens were toffs from Agatha Christie.

In a landscape so flat, a view of the sea might seem commonplace: every villager's right. But scarcely anyone—the Elstons included—could see the waves from their windows behind the sandy embankment. A sea view at Chapel was, and remains, expensive, available only from a private road that runs up and along a fortified stretch of the ridge.

Walking humbly past with my mother on the road to the village from our lower lying house, I would gaze up at my uncle's mansion, called with some élan The Beacon. He had his own tennis court. When I was old enough, some vague invitation was issued to go and play. But when my friend Pat and I had the courage to turn up, it was made mortifyingly clear that we were rather a nuisance, that the court had not yet been marked out with the white roller that day. We were in awe, too, of the one car in our narrow world, which of course belonged to the Captain. Bicycles were the only wheeled transport in Chapel in the Thirties. It was a suave polished Humber with a curved boot lid, in which I never once rode. As a young nobody I knew my place, and was slowly becoming aware of the resentments between Veda and Hilda.

A period guidebook to Chapel makes a feature of this gleaming vehicle, pictured in a suitably empty landscape in all its unrivaled glory.

Veda and Hilda were two of nine children born to John and Rebecca Crawford. Three died young, including the baby before Hilda, who was also named Hilda. Some were born in the nearby village of Hogsthorpe, where John Crawford sold "cattle and victuals," according to the 1881 census; the others were born in Chapel, where the Crawfords managed the Vine until his death at the age of forty-six. A photograph from 1892 of Rebecca in funeral clothes shows her holding John's photograph, the shadow of one person's life within that of another, memento inside memento. Veda was her first child, patient and gentle. Hilda was her last, and supposedly the luckiest, with the great good fortune to marry Captain Green. Outwardly respected in Chapel, he was privately regarded as an impossible snob, not least because he never relinquished his officer title. For all his military bearing and matching toothbrush moustache, Green had achieved this rank merely through desk duty in the Indian army, whereas other villagers had seen active service in the trenches of the First World War. A white marble cross outside the church lists the glorious dead of that war and the next. Thirty-seven men died from this hamlet alone. It is well said that no British village was untouched.

Like many ex-officers, Captain Green stayed on in India, running a trading business in the Raj. Its legacy survives in our family even today. The Indian cotton sheets he brought back as a present for Veda in 1920 became my parents' wedding linen thirty years later; they have lasted into the twenty-first century with only the slightest mending. My daughter has a seal carved from the tusk of an Indian elephant dead a century ago. A cabin trunk somehow came down to my mother. With its wooden hoops and striped madras interior, it looks like a prop from *A Passage to India*. I had it as a student, and it held everything I owned for several years afterwards. Such are the vagaries of family memory that only now does it strike me that the initials HG painted on its side must have signified Captain Green.

Unless, of course, the trunk belonged to Hugh Green, the Captain's young son. The Greens had two children, Hugh and Rebe, older than Betty by eight and ten years respectively. Perhaps this was the luggage of a boarding-school boy, so rarely home that my mother doesn't remember her big cousin at all. There was very little chance to get to know him, moreover, for his life was appallingly short. Hugh left school at eighteen and immediately volunteered for the navy in the Second World War. He was assigned to a fleet and sailed away to war; or so it was said. For a long time there was no news of him; and the months eventually turned to years without a single word or sighting. His is the final name at the foot of the Chapel church cross: *Hugh Green—Navy*. Another soul who went to sea and never came back.

Captain Green was a restless man. He had barely returned to the Beacon before the view from the panoramic windows would lure him straight back overseas. I have inherited an album of postcards he sent to the very young Rebe, casually remarking, as if it were quite insignificant, that her parents are yet again elsewhere. One from Selfridges Hotel on Oxford Street says, "Dear little baby, we are going to visit friends. We shall come back on Saturday, or perhaps Tuesday. Hoping you are a good girl." *Helping Daddy*, as another is captioned, shows a ribboned moppet doing up the laces of her adored father's boots before he sets off; apt, since the Captain is now in India. A puppy from 1919 bears this message: "Dear Baby, Daddy leaves in a Big Ship tomorrow. Look after Mummy." He is on his way to Egypt and Palestine. Business is booming. In the summer of 1920 he writes from Delhi to his four-year-old daughter, "I hope you are having a jolly time each day on the beach, but not paddling like the little girl on the other side of this card!" This vulgar child is showing her sunburnt knees.

Granny Crawford must be looking after Rebe, as practically every other postcard in the album is a covert message to her. Occasionally the news is worrying. Hilda writes from London: "I have not heard from Daddy. Indian Cavalry in action it says in today's *Mirror*, tell Granny." But the Captain lived to see another deal; and Rebe gained a shiny new spade for Chapel Sands from the generosity born of relief.

As she got older, Rebe accompanied Hilda to London to buy clothes from the distant sophistication of Marshall & Snelgrove on Oxford Street. Their purchases were a great focus of my mother's longing.

Aunt Hilda's impeccably matched ensembles were unequalled, pure Country House couture, and she wore the finest triple pearls that made me long for a little glamour. But it was all complicated by class and money, and by the refusal of my mother to compete, even if she could ever have afforded it. Hilda would occasionally hand over a dress-box containing some discarded gown in many sheets of tissue paper to poor sister Veda, and my mother would be incensed and refuse the costly contents. I remember the rejection scenes when they were examined and discovered to be totally useless, grand finery, often in black silk, a colour Veda never wore and I expect regarded by her and the village as funeral garments. I was not so proud and begged my cousin once to lend me an exquisite pair of green velvet shoes for an evening, merely to totter about in high heels to feel exotic. They were fit for a princess, and hard to give back. I was eight to Rebe's eighteen.

Once, much later in the 1960s, when my father sold a painting and was temporarily flush, he urged my mother to buy some new shoes. They became a family legend: the most expensive things she ever owned, worn for every special occasion for forty years until they disappeared, stolen from her hotel room the day after my wedding. The lost shoes were, of course, green.

Betty was in uncomfortable awe of Cousin Rebe all her life and appalled when I accidentally shattered a china terrier in Rebe's (all-green) house as a child. My brother and I were also supposed to creep about in humble respect. Rebe once took us to tea at a grand hotel where we were urged to eat our cake with a knife and fork so that no crumbs would be shed on our clothes, an etiquette we found bizarre. But it stirred some kind of Chapel nostalgia in my mother, which in turn agonized me. I later saved up my wages as a teenage shop assistant to buy her the elegant tea knives she never had.

In the Elston house, everything about eating seemed rude. "Don't play with it. Don't push it about. Don't be slow/leave food/ scrape the plate/talk with your mouth full/say you don't want it/say you want more of it/slump over the table/make eating noises. Sit up straight, elbows down in velvet silence, chew without showing your teeth."

I picture Betty pushing miserably at some remaining morsel under her parents' watchful eyes. Or perhaps it is a thick white glue of ground rice known as Aunt Jackson's pudding. "How I despised Aunt Jackson who had originally devised this pulp and written the recipe into my mother's book in sloping copperplate script, faded sepia now but still ensuring that her culinary dictatorship survived beyond the grave."

When she was eight, my mother was required to eat a plate of something noxious with the appetite-choking name of fish custard in front of the whole school at Miss Turney's. Everyone else had finished; they all waited, and waited. Punishment was threatened. Eventually she forced it down, only for the custard to return immediately. Food is fear. One incident leaves its stain over more than eight decades. In a restaurant, a lifetime later, my mother scolded her grandchildren just as sharply as George ever did, I suspect, for not finishing every scrap (and for ordering too much) while failing to eat her own dinner. She apologized profusely to the waiter, to the point of imploring his forgiveness and even that of the chef, while simultaneously mounting a self-defense to the effect that she had been given too big a portion. She is both George and herself at such moments. I have never left a plate unfinished in my life, no matter what it holds; I have inherited the fear, and the reproaches.

My daughter Thea, on hearing the fish custard tale around the age of twelve, laughed at the Dickensian scene and its unending consequences: "Grandma, I wouldn't have cared about that for more than a day!" But she has never feared a tyrant across the dinner table. And perhaps, in another life, my mother would have been just as blithely unabashed. It makes me wonder, once more: What is my mother's own true nature, and what is the life she has been dealt, the tide of daily events that knocked her back and forth, that she swims in, or tries to swim in? If I could discover how she lived in those first unknown years, what her original world was like before the Elstons, I feel I might find a difference between Grace and Betty.

Paralyzing social anxiety arrived early for both my mother and me. What made her so fearful; did her fearfulness shape mine? My earliest memory of the world outside my childhood home is of being taken to a Christmas party at a church nursery school when I was three. There were the familiar Scottish Episcopalian staff. There were the red-haired identical twins who lived up the road. But I knew nobody else and terror coursed through me. I did not know how to speak to strangers, though they were only children; I did not know how to dispose my limbs, carry my person, where or how to stand in the room. Turning to find my mother gone, I felt tears compounding the shame. But there was one saving grace: the door that had been my entrance might also be my exit. I ran out of the church, only to find myself in the alarming darkness of a December afternoon with no idea where I was. Then I saw the beautiful cascades of water that glittered down the inside of the local fish shop window, some kind of automatic cleansing that occurred daily at 5 p.m. and which we children always hoped to witness. Goldenacre was the name of this unlovely granite district of Edinburgh, and I confused the name with the shop with the fish, so that somehow the window streams with goldfish in my memory. Extreme fear is amazingly open to these comforting distractions. I don't know how I got home, except that it did not involve returning to the party.

My mother, allowed to go nowhere, longing to do so, was eventually rewarded with her first party invitation at the Sunday school where she received strict lessons and the Holy Land stamps to lick for the attendance book. It was a dim and chilly walk along the lanes and over the dark dikes to church; but at least there were other children, among them two siblings called Gabrielle and Michael.

They were the beautiful people who once had a Christmas party to which I was invited. I had no idea how to behave, and what did I do but bow deeply on shaking hands with Michael, aged about 6 or 7, knowing immediately that it was a huge gaffe. Staring and sniggering faces and my own mortification at having acted on some impulse from goodness knows where . . . And I have ever since suffered the same awkward embarrassment that another gaffe is about to be performed at every social occasion. The fear is well below the surface of course, for a lifetime of learning that one does not bow, one behaves thus or thus, like everyone else, has gradually been acquired. Yet it is still there.

Despite—or because of—all this, my mother puts every visitor at their ease, welcomes everyone in. But at such perverse cost: a headache preceded every social gathering at our house, when I was growing up. I can remember her lying down for a day before, and sometimes a day after, the annual dinner at the Royal Scottish Academy. She kept a notebook of food cooked for other people over the years in case she ever committed the solecism of feeding them the same thing twice. To be ready for an event involved—still involves—weeks of anticipation. To avoid being late means being many hours early.

She threw a momentous party for my seventh birthday. It took place in a garage, transformed into an underwater lagoon with nets of paper fish hanging from the ceiling and tables covered in what looked like shining blue water, a brilliant hand-painted illusion. There were starfish biscuits and jellies in the shape of salmon; these marvels eclipse all the fear of it in my memory. For my brother there was a birthday cake in the form of a soccer pitch with tiny goals, all the colors ingeniously blended out of the primitive food dyes available in 1970s Edinburgh. Best of all was a Halloween cake made to resemble the barrel of floating apples for which we would later dook, biting them out of the water with hands tied behind our backs. These facsimile fruits were marzipan, made to look exactly like miniature Cox's Orange Pippins. My mother worked the colors with a fine hog's-hair brush, just as she did when actually painting. To me, this cake exceeded anything in "The Baker's Daughter."

Only imagine how unusual this was in a capital city where you could scarcely buy garlic or peppers and silver balls were the only cake decorations. My English mother, arriving in Edinburgh as an art student in 1948, was staggered to hear the dustmen working on Christmas Day. It was, and remained for her, a closed and puritanical city.

The salmon jelly was made from a mold that had once belonged to Veda, and Granny Crawford before her. There is a print of the very same object in *Mrs. A.B. Marshall's Book of Cookery*, from 1888, alongside the result turned out, so that I can see as a graphic image exactly what three generations of my family ate. The picture is an opening to that long-ago past when they had to fiddle about with gelatin, boiled water, and cochineal to come up with a lifelike salmon. Through it I see Mrs. Crawford in the kitchens at the Vine, and Veda working away with her paraffin stove for a special occasion—images once again a prism for life.

The Elstons and the Greens did not eat together, or even drink tea. They scarcely seem to have encountered each other at all, despite living not half a mile apart. "Once I remember Uncle Hugh bringing a sack of mussels and spending an evening with my father, making merry with the sea food and drinking Guinness," my mother wrote. "The two men sat there working open the shiny black shells. I think there was an air of disapproval from Veda at this Rabelaisian scene. But they were, of course, never friends, and it was plain that we were considered well beneath them."

That sense of hierarchy reproduced itself in our rare encounters with Cousin Rebe, my mother's anxiety transmitting so directly to me that I was too afraid of saying the wrong thing to speak at all. But beneath my cowed speechlessness was a mounting rebellion: Why were we to be quite so servile to this woman, a domestic science teacher at a girls' public school, when my mother was an actual artist? And what was so remarkable about Captain Green, who was a kind of traveling salesman himself, except that he made so much more money than George? Suppression thwarts precision. I have never felt able to represent myself in speech, only through the merciful slowness and forgiving second chances of writing. My mother, on the other hand, both speaks and writes with an enquiring generosity that drew children as well as adults to our house when I was young; they became my friends, I feel, because of her.

Trying to discover the character of Chapel in those prewar times, I sifted through years of local newspapers. And it was in the *Skegness Times*, the biggest publication for miles around, that I came across the tale of a controversial church meeting. "Chapel Parish Outrage" tells of the vicar's scandalous snobbery at the Christmas party of 1944. The vicar sat at high table with Captain and Mrs. Green and the local gentry; much farther down the hall were the local children and their mothers, and farther still the brass cleaners, including Veda. The article quotes at length from the minutes of the meeting. These record an impressive uprising against the vicar, who had doled out the food with outrageous discrimination—chocolate cakes and cream blancmanges for his table, wartime jelly and plain biscuits for the children. He had also failed to award Sunday-school prizes for the second year running, with the implication that he was pocketing the money. The dialogue is remarkably dramatic, building to a violent crossfire of biblical quotations, and the entire proceedings were leaked to the paper, where they appeared on the front page. Veda took the minutes (her voice is never heard in them). I would like to think that she secretly exposed the vicar's snobbery to the press.

I feel mutinous still about the relationship between Hilda and Veda. Their sisterliness, though a fact, did not exist in feeling. How was it possible for Hilda to bypass Veda at church gatherings and even drive right past her without a word in the street? Inexplicable to me, too, is the strange truth that Granny Crawford, in old age, presumably having served her purpose as nanny to Hilda's children, went to live with Veda in a cramped house with a bullying son-in-law, tight rations, and no money, instead of rising up to the elegant Beacon; to that vast house with its views across the water to Europe, where maids came to clean the eight bedrooms, half of them empty, housekeepers kept perfect order and special food was brought up by train from Fortnum & Mason in London. Money and class were apparently what divided these households, and turned me into a raging teenage socialist on Veda's behalf. I admire her proud rejection of the cast-off silk garments. Equally, I wish the Beacon hadn't set up such a pattern of longing in my mother: for an indoor bathroom or a pair of shoes. A sense of deprivation might never have occurred in her young life if there had not been this house, and this family, hoisted up there on the top of the dunes, condescending to the Elstons with their hand-me-downs.

I do not know whether Betty was regarded as a proper niece by the Greens, or just a rather sudden and random addition to the Elston household. Betty was excelling at school, which may have softened their attitude and given Veda some protective pride of her own. But life at the Beacon was never as lucky as it looked to the Elstons from St. Leonard's Villas.

Hugh Green did join the navy, but was soon after dismissed in undisclosed circumstances, to the horror of his father. It was then that he vanished. His parents could not believe he was lost at sea. Perhaps he was still alive and simply somewhere else in the world. His mother watched the beach for his returning figure, and for years left a note for him on the hall table every time she went out. And Rebe, their admired daughter, who had the flouncy dresses, velvet shoes, and elaborate cakes from London, who went to birthday parties everywhere, never married as her parents hoped. She taught cookery and games at a school in nearby Horncastle, where my mother occasionally encountered her older cousin during hockey matches. Her chief pleasures, as it seemed to us, lay in fine linen tablecloths, proper scones, and the collection of china dogs that came to us after her death, along with the little rabbit-fur cloak she had worn to those childhood parties. Rebe retired to a bungalow about ten miles from the great house of her childhood. Captain Green, eventually persuaded that his son was dead, ensured that Hugh's name was inscribed on the cross, before gradually fading away.

The cake was cardboard for them all, as it would not be for Betty.

She may have been the Carmelita Miggs who longed for the dresses, the shoes, and the social poise; but for Rebe, who had everything, these things proved inconsequential. Yet she did have one precious possession that her cousin did not, and that was knowledge. Rebe knew who Betty Elston was.

5

The Town

At the age of ten, my mother won a scholarship to Skegness Grammar, and the radius of her life suddenly became seven miles wider. George's pride in her academic gifts trumped his jailer's instincts, and she was allowed to take the bus to school on her own. Perhaps he thought Betty would be safer outside the narrow village circle, that there would be safety in numbers in this venerable institution with its three hundred pupils. He was wrong.

Exactly how my mother achieved this modicum of freedom is a marvel in another way, for she came from a house as lacking in books as images. Her parents read no further than a daily paper and the church magazine. The oak shelf in the parlor remained empty except for the Bible, a romantic novel from 1921, and a school prize awarded by Miss Turney that seemed even more hopeless to Betty than the Bible, although its author was another first-line genius. "Marley was dead, to begin with"—six chilling words that put her off Dickens's *A Christmas Carol* for years. "Ghostly Marley and wretched Scrooge haunted my Decembers all the same; their chains clanked and their voices spooled over the ether, as my parents listened in with relish to this annual treat on the wireless." My own childhood was exhilaratingly haunted in turn, as my mother dramatized the story so that everyone in our family had several roles. The last theater performance she saw before deafness set in was Simon Callow's magnificent adaptation in which he plays all the parts. No show has ever meant more to me because it meant so much to her, bringing her life full circle.

In one of his photographs, taken for a Christmas card, George posed Betty in the crook of a tree holding up a book called *Happy Days*. "I remember hating it all, the artificial smile, the sitting quite still for an eternity, eyes watering in the sunlight, while my father got his picture. How amazed he would have been to have known my feelings running so contrary to the slogan." So much of her young life involved these sustained and gallant performances.

Happy Days was an anthology of short stories and verse, mostly trite, but it did include a few extracts from Shakespeare, which is how my mother was able to recognize *A Midsummer Night's Dream* as the source of the proclamation written above the arch to Butlin's

first holiday camp on the Skegness road. It is still there: OUR TRUE INTENT IS ALL FOR YOUR DELIGHT. She had, moreover, played the part of Mustardseed while at Miss Turney's. Like so many children, her whole education seems to have been ignited by one inspirational teacher from early childhood: Miss Turney's assistant, who lent her books, and even helped her to send off for them by post; they came in brown-paper parcels all the way from Lincoln County Library.

George seems to have believed that books were an impediment to learning—"Got your nose in a book again," he would complain.

But the possibilities of Skegness Grammar were not lost upon him, and the Chapel dressmaker was commissioned to turn out a thrifty semblance of the school uniform in yellow and green. And off my mother went, one year younger than her fellow pupils and exceedingly nervous, to this historic red-brick school.

Skegness in 1936 was a lively and elegant resort. The wide yellow beach was as flat as the bowling green and the ornamental gardens, with their scented roses and winding pergola paths. The grandly named shorefront hotels—Chatsworth, Park Lane, the Savoy—opened their doors to Midlands bankers and lawyers. Boardinghouses with cheerful striped awnings welcomed Derby miners, Liverpool dockers, and young secretaries up from London for the sun. As the railways got faster, the tickets cheaper, and the workers' holidays longer, following the 1926 General Strike, more and more visitors returned each year to the so-called Garden City by the Sea, so that the population swelled sixfold every summer for the promise of "a champagne bath to re-energise the body, and champagne air to fill the lungs." The Suncastle pleasure palace, with its faux-medieval turrets, opened for tea dances; the big Ferris wheel ground into action, its swings fashioned to look like brightly colored hot-air balloons. The putting green, miniature railway, and fairy dell pool for infants appeared and are all still there, just as traces of Edwardian grandeur survive in the wide avenues and balconied houses.

On the beachfront now, the blue paintwork fades to white and a sudden shaft of winter sun strikes the dun sea, emphasizing the fine silver brush-line that divides the monochrome sky from the monochrome water. Glowing lightbulbs sway uneasily along the front. People walk their dogs miles away, as it seems, at the sea's edge while the big wheel slowly turns. Skegness, off-season, still has the power to enchant, a period piece of the pleasurable past. And on hoardings all over town, the fat figure of the Jolly Fisherman still jaunts along the beach in his wellington boots, arms merrily outflung, in John Hassall's imperishable 1908 poster. There he goes, skipping over a starfish, beneath the slogan that helped to make the resort popular: *Skegness is SO bracing!* He will be here forever, long after the visitors have dwindled away, lured abroad by cheaper spots and less bracing weather.

Coming into school on the bus from Chapel, Betty traveled

through the flatlands of brassica fields and shining dikes, past road-side cherry stalls and the gradual blossoming of Ingoldmells from hamlet to early caravan village. In that same year, 1936, Amy Johnson, the first woman to fly solo from England to Australia, cut the red ribbon for Butlin's new holiday camp, with its neat avenues of chalets, its amateur dramatics and cockcrow gymnastics. The iron traceries of Butlin's roller coasters still rise in towering corkscrews above the landscape, dark ink sketches scribbled against the marine sky. The bus sees them long in advance, and draws in at the gate every morning for chefs, entertainers, and ice cream sellers to alight for the day's work. These passengers come from Anderby, Con-ingsby, Hundleby, Firsby, even Tennyson's Somersby: the village names are pure Viking. Children from these places, so romantic to my mother's mind, also streamed into Skegness Grammar.

In summer, the sky is almost blindingly bright, arcing high above the green crops. In winter, voluminous clouds scud blue-black over bare claggy soil. Even now the nameless roads are only just wide enough for tractors and hay carts, twisting around the boundaries of ancient fields, barely any distance between sharp right-angled bends. Sugar beet alternates with potatoes—the Second World War victory crop—brussels sprouts with beans, sending out their beautiful fragrance into the summer air. Dikes cross with drains; black soil abounds when the level fields lie fallow. Even the hedges are low, and in my mother's part of the county, there are not even any woods for a poet to praise.

Gradually Betty began to draw what she saw from the bus, trying hard to get down the peculiar geography: "I faced the obvious pitfalls: how to express the vastness of the plain stretching away to the horizon, unfeatured almost, and the nebulous over-circling hemisphere, to make it all breathe, make the space limitlessly airy and never inert." At school, the art teacher, who would later become a decisive figure in my mother's life, showed her Rembrandt's etchings. "He could do this with the Dutch landscape in such a few deft lines incised on the copper plate. I wondered why we had no

Rembrandt. One quarter of Lincolnshire, after all, was even named Holland." She never saw Joseph Crawhall's paintings of dikes and drains reflecting the wintry Lincolnshire light, or John Sell Cotman's windmills rising like dark giants against the clouds, with their cutting-shafting-whirring sails, tiny figures below sometimes gazing up at the spectacle. British art was scarcely mentioned at school, and never, of course, at home.

With the exception of art classes, embarrassment colored most of my mother's school days. She felt shy, by far the youngest in any class, and could never answer a question without turning red, a display unkindly remarked upon by the science teacher to explain the meaning of the term *properties* to his pupils. "That girl's property," he would say, pointing at her, "is the property of continuous blushing." Blushing begets blushing, of course; like insomnia or self-consciousness, it catches itself happening and keeps reproducing itself.

The teachers from those times are more vivid than my own through her telling. The wonderful English mistress Anne Brackenridge, ending long discussions of Tennyson's poetry with her rousing catchphrase "On then!" We say it still, when stalled or tired. Annie Brack taught her class Dickens's *Bleak House*, in which Lincolnshire itself makes an appearance, rare in the work of any other English novelist. Lady Dedlock lives in Lincolnshire, or one might say is slowly dying of misery there, in this dank countryside "of low-lying ground, with stagnant rivers and melancholy trees for islands in them, and a surface punctured all over, all day long, with falling rain."

Much later in life, in a letter to me, my mother wondered whether Lincolnshire could in fact be fertile ground for creativity.

I believe that the land upon which one lives influences one's character. Tennyson is always aware of its multitude of possibilities for mood analogies: the opposing character, for instance, of the static plain and the never-still waters.

The drain-cut levels of the marshy lea—
Gray sand banks, and pale sunset—dreary wind,
Dim shores, dense rains, and heavy-clouded sea.

But I'm a prose person, so I plod on—or plough on. Instantly I see the flat brown fields and the heavy cart horses, it's always blowing—the sea and the land level and like-coloured. But Tennyson made poetry of it. I delight in his poems rather than the reality; this, art can do.

It never occurs to her that there might be art in her own words. She considers herself as gloomy as the land; and yet to strangers, friends, and children, above all her own, she is as celebratory as summer, appreciative of every image and word, of every encounter and conversation. The inner and the outer do not match.

At school my mother found freedom in the lessons, with all their news of elsewhere and their intellectual independence from home. In her first school reports, the teachers were mildly surprised to find that she seemed to have "an unusual aptitude for art." She was allowed to use the art room at lunchtime and encouraged to enter competitions. In her third year there, she won a national prize for a poster promoting Lincolnshire, like John Hassall before her. It must have featured the landscape, she believes, though the memory has since dissolved. In her fourth year, she appeared in the school play alongside the very same science teacher who had mocked her for blushing.

I had been chosen, inexplicably, for a part in a very Lincolnshire production named *El Dorado*. This was the name of a potato newly introduced into the county and notable for its prolific tenacity. My role was to be a feckless farmer's daughter who inadvertently cooks the very precious, first seed El Dorados. I remember crossing the stage with a large pan full of bones for the farm dog. I was to lift the latch and throw them outside. Opening the door I found Mr. Porter crouched down below giving very large barks. I couldn't suppress my laughter at this ludicrous reversal. It was strange that he had cast me in that role at all, on the grounds that I was the only one who could project loud enough to be heard at the furthest end of the school hall, in contrast to my inaudible mumbles in class.

We hide behind other people's words, lose our self-consciousness in playing someone else. The stage, at that time, was less anxious than real life.

She made lasting friendships at Skegness Grammar, discovered that other people's family lives could be quite different from her own, occasionally even went to stay in their houses at weekends and visit the cinema with them to watch Charlie Chaplin's *The Great Dictator* and Hitchcock's *Rebecca*. She stitched a calico sunsuit based on a poster of the film star Deanna Durbin; I have it still: yellow, the color of hope. She must have worn it on the beach in summer, on those smooth flat sands that run all the way from Chapel to Skegness, no shelving, no sudden undertow, the beach huts beginning to gather in parades along the Skegness foreshore, twenty shillings a week with gas rings, drop tables, and the fresh spray of the waves. Edna White's Ladies Orchestra played thés dansants daily at the Suncastle. A lioness escaped from the zoo, briefly marauding Molly's Beach Café. Billy Butlin released an Indian elephant onto the sands, where it walked along in a glittering howdah, a colossus visible for miles along the shore.

At school they were taught Tennyson without ever learning that he came from nearby Somersby and walked these same beaches. There was even a Tennyson House, to which Betty belonged, and another named after Isaac Newton. The hockey team went to play matches in Spilsby without ever being told that this was the birthplace of the great explorer Sir John Franklin, who set off to discover the Northwest Passage in 1845 and disappeared without a trace. Betty did not know that Franklin was from Lincolnshire, any more than Newton, or the revolutionary philosopher Thomas Paine. In later life, she longed for someone to have come from her county besides the boatmen and brassica farmers, and there were so many more than she realized. Captain John Smith of Willoughby, a hamlet on the farthest edge of the circuit she was allowed to cycle, left that tiny spot on the globe to become an explorer, founded the Virginia Colony, and mapped the New England coast. Smith sailed the high seas as both captain and pirate; he was sold as a slave but later knighted by the Prince of Transylvania. His life was saved by Pocahontas, but then nearly lost to French pirates on the way home from the Americas. His remains lie buried in St. Sepulchre-without-Newgate in London, where a stained-glass window honoring his memory was installed in 1968. It proposes, with bathetic understatement, that he was the most notable person to have come out of Willoughby. Smith was educated at the grammar school in Louth, a few miles from Chapel; so were Tennyson and Franklin.

Franklin was a bullied child, constantly abused by his father for being too dreamy and slow. The boy longed always to be somewhere else. Repeatedly, he tried to get away from the strict confines of home to reach the sea, running all the way from Spilsby to the coast. He once got as far as the beach at Ingoldmells, a mile from Chapel, only to be discovered and severely beaten. Betty often passed this spot on her bicycle, knowing it only because this was where a crazy man lurked who liked to put his stick between the spokes of children's wheels. Franklin's niece Emily married Tennyson, who would in turn write an epitaph for the lost explorer, long after he disappeared.

The headmaster of Skegness Grammar was a dignified man named K. G. Spendlove, revered by all, including the local newspapers where he appears as the voice of reason and paragon of academic authority. In the course of my mother's first year at the school, he sent a letter home asking all parents to produce their children's birth certificates in relation to a new polio vaccine. She dutifully handed the letter to George, knowing exactly what it contained. But nothing was given for her to take back. No birth certificate was produced; and nobody explained why. In fact, the Elstons did not have it. To his daughter's embarrassment, George had to take the bus into Skegness for a private interview with Mr. Spendlove in order to maintain some kind of strange secrecy. Betty was filled with shame.

The school day at Skegness Grammar ended at 4 p.m. In summer, my mother was sometimes allowed to cycle back home, but never in any other season. Nor was she allowed to linger in Skegness after classes, walk on the sands with friends, or eat sundaes at Molly's café. There was only one bus back to Chapel on weekday afternoons, and no second chance if she missed it. Towards the end of the day's lessons, she would grow tense, worrying that the teachers might go on talking after the bell, that the corridors would be impassably crammed, that someone might intervene between the school gate and the rush to the bus stop. Her exit from Skegness had to be swift, prompt, and decisive, contributing to a lifetime's dread of being late. Except for school, the town was a no-go zone, visited only for the dentist or the one department store where regulation shoes were bought in Veda's company. But at least Betty could run through the streets between school and bus on her own without encountering any kind of danger, without anyone spying or interfering, or so George believed; in fact, people were watching her all the time. Worse still was the green country bus, where she was both vulnerable to the public and trapped in close confines. George does not seem to have considered this risk. But it was on this bus that Betty's life divided.

6

The Bus

"Your grandmother wants to see you."

I sat there in numb disbelief on hearing these words. The surrounding buzz of boys and girls fell suddenly silent. I was the focus of everyone's attention. The children around me on the bus were about as amazed as I was to hear this bewildering statement. For I had no grandmother.

The woman had come down the aisle towards the seat where I was sitting with my schoolfriend Pat—an elderly woman, as it seemed to me, dressed in black with a squashed felt hat and hair pinned in a bun beneath it. A villager on her way home from town with her cumbersome shopping, a countrywoman I had seen many times—and she clearly me—but who had never before addressed me. She held up a small shadowy photograph of my infant self. How could she possibly have it?

I said nothing and turned immediately away, as one turns from great shame or madness. It was a moment of pure shock, of such stunning silent force that I felt only panic, a need to get out of that place and run home, shutting the door behind me and never more emerge to a world that could terrify me with sudden crazy confrontations. I do not know what she did next, I only remember being desperate to get away from this terrible moment, to get free and rush home to my mother.

But when I did get to the house, my mother—my only mother—was standing at the stove as usual and continued to stir the pot while I repeated the mad woman's words. She remained calm while I cried and questioned. Veda said nothing, did nothing, in no way tried to comfort me. All she proposed was that I should go out and ride my bicycle. I was thirteen years old.

My mother remembers nothing of the bicycle ride, has no idea how long she was gone. But when she returns, George has somehow arrived on the scene. They take her into the little parlor, with its Willow pattern china and its unused fireplace, sit her down, and take up their position on the opposite sofa.

To her amazement, they do not begin with the grandmother who wanted to see her, or the woman on the bus, or her relationship to Betty. They say nothing at all about the photograph (now or ever). They do not try to reassure their daughter, or give any kind of rational understanding of what has occurred. All George offers is that they "took her in" as a small child long ago, and that they are in fact her adopted parents. But the main thrust of his instruction, which will stay with her forever, is a renewed emphasis on isolation—with the onus on Betty. She must not speak to this woman ever again.

The cold news in the parlor shattered her stability, the whole basis of her identity gone in an instant. She lost her footing completely. And my mother felt this way—nameless, unmoored, apart—all through her life until her own children were born; it seems to me that she still feels this in relation to other people. She has had a hundred friends, loved and cherished them all, and almost forty years of marriage to my father until his death, but it is her children who matter. "I never belonged to anyone," she once wrote to me, "until I belonged to you." And also, "You are my most precious possession." For years I did not understand this last phrase, straining away from its connotations of objects and ownership—until I learned her story.

It is incredible that George managed to deliver this devastating news in the form of a never-ending threat. The woman in black was often on the bus. Betty had noticed her before, and would likely see her again. How was she to avoid the situation, and in any case why was she reproached for speaking to this lady when she had remained entirely mute? The Elstons' rule could not possibly be enforced, and yet it hung over her always. This woman who had been watching her might come down the aisle again.

The Elstons lived near a significant little construction called Tyler's Bridge. It crossed what the Dutch call a sluice and the English a drain—a narrow, muddy wash that meandered down to the sea past her house. It is typical of the coastal fens. The drain itself already held past horror because of the night that Veda's friend Mrs. Ailsby had gone out of her house in the darkness, tripped into the drain, and drowned.

Tyler's was the place where Betty escaped the bus to hurtle home. This place that had once been such a simple stop on the trundling single-decker route now seemed ringed with menace. She might have to brush past the woman to get out. No other way home—no cars, no possible lifts; the one-and-only bus now held other terrors.

My mother at last had a friend, Pat Richardson, who also traveled back and forth to Skegness Grammar. Pat said nothing during or after this incident. Inadequate as this seems to me—how could she possibly fail to come up with some words, some kind of response?—what is worse is that she actually understood what was happening. Pat had heard of Betty's grandmother, knew where she lived and who she was. And Pat was not the only one. I see that scene on the bus, the faces all around Betty, the people of Chapel, many of them just children: decades later, we learned that most of them knew of her origins, as did their parents, and quite probably the proverbial dogs in the street. Nobody hinted, or broke down and told, yet each knew far more about Betty than she knew herself. The irony is dramatic, the tiny traveling community like a chorus to the forthcoming tragedy.

Also on this fateful bus was a legal secretary called Miss Moore, returning from her job in Skegness. She knew my mother somewhat, being the niece of the Chapel seamstress who stitched her school clothes. Veda, in her kindness, had once paid for identical summer dresses to be made for Betty and her doll. Standing on a chair for fittings, Betty would occasionally see Miss Moore slipping past through the corridors in the seamstress's house. She had an impression of pinched and premature age. Half a century on, we discovered that Kathleen Moore knew all about it too—indeed, she knew very intimately why this woman had approached Betty Elston on the bus, and precisely who her grandmother was, for in her previous job, she had personally handled the adoption document.

When my mother managed to acquire this heavy piece of parchment many years later, in the 1960s, she was chilled to see the secretary's signature there as a witness. Miss Moore had known all about her origins, and had turned away in the seat where she generally sat, next to the woman in black.

Betty's life changed in an instant. But it need not have turned out as it did. George and Veda could have reacted differently, as kinder parents might. Instead of casting Betty as a waif and stray charitably rescued, they could have told her that she was their daughter and they loved her, that her arrival had turned them into a family. They could have told her that adoption was common, that they had been hoping and praying for her to come; that she did have a grandmother who also loved her, but lived somewhere else, and that this particular situation was complicated. They could even have told her that there was an adopted child living two doors away, that it was quite normal and indeed known to the boy himself. But the conversation in the parlor was over in moments. It was followed by an iron silence.

Veda and George were noticeably older than all the other parents. Betty had always wondered why; now she understood. And this knowledge became a kind of shield against them. "I moved away from my parents at this point. Nobody had anything to say to me, so I said nothing to them. I had spent much of my life feeling frightened of my father, now I felt cut off from all feeling connected with him. I had a complete loss of affection, perhaps to protect myself in some way from these people who scarcely seemed to want to own me. I was not of them."

Something of this was perhaps a typical teenage reaction. We are nothing like our parents; how can we even be related to them—perhaps we are secretly adopted? And so it strangely turns out, almost by way of explanation for the absence of feeling on both sides. Betty began to dislike George intensely. It was a full stop to innocence.

Much later, when I was myself a teenager, my mother was in an Edinburgh department store taking a lift to the top floor when the mechanism jammed. The passengers were stuck for almost two hours. Afterwards she became acutely claustrophobic, and for years could not bear to be in any small space. A specialist at the Royal Infirmary eventually broke the spell with much gentle practice in and out of lifts. He also identified the cause of her panic—not the intelligent fear of being trapped, fainting, the air running out, and so on, but my mother's reaction to the other people in the lift, a group of blue-rinse Edinburgh matrons who maintained a rigid silence throughout. She wanted to scream, to appeal to them, to have the comfort of a mutual response that never came, but was increasingly afraid of breaching the decorum. For the lift, read the green bus.

For some time after that journey, she suffered from a recurrent nightmare: "I was once again in a bus, once again fearful, once again desperate to escape. This time my way was barred by a woman seated in the only doorway, immovable, shelling a basket of peas. There may be something symbolic in the splitting of peas, the revealing of concealed contents in the dream. But my memory reveals much more—that I am once again trapped and frightened by a person unknown."

My mother has written this episode several times over the years, turning it over as if to discover some new meaning within it. Only once, in the birthday memoir, does she mention the small photograph of herself as a child. It seems to me that she both saw it and did not see it, remembering only the shock of recognition for a fraction of a second before looking away. But it is significant that she registered her own face in that instant; it cannot have been a family photograph, in which she would have had to pick herself out of a crowd. It must have been a solo portrait, black and white. This photograph was decisive proof, the single clearest way that the woman in black could demonstrate the truth of what she was saying—that there was an earlier life and another family elsewhere, that Betty had another grandmother before Chapel, and before Granny Crawford.

The birthday memoir does not go many years beyond the age of thirteen, the age my mother was when the woman approached her with the picture and the shattering news. Indeed, this was almost all she knew when she sat down to write the memoir for me at the age of fifty-six, still in a state of ignorance about the kidnap, her first mother, or any other family. These revelations were all yet to come.

The woman on the bus turned out to be one of her own relatives. I have always respected her wisdom in coming down the aisle with the photograph as ocular proof of Betty's early life. She needed documentary evidence to gain her attention, and how else could she back up this unthinkable claim? But she never again approached my mother, always continuing her journey to the next and final stop on the route, the nearby village of Hogsthorpe.

"Your grandmother wants to see you." About this forebear, my mother seems to have been numbly incurious at the time. And in the many years of returning to this moment, she has never wondered why it was the grandmother and not the mother whose proxy approached her on the bus. When she became a grandmother herself, however, she began to think how much hurt was suffered by the one who wanted to see her and how much anguish could have been spared if only it had come to pass. To the thirteen-year-old Betty, however, this grandmother was horrifyingly surreal, "a kind of living ghost."

And who was this woman? My mother would not discover her identity for another thirty years. All she knew now was that George and Veda were not her father and mother as she had always thought. Except that even this was not the truth.

7

George and Veda

A photograph exists of the Elstons swinging along on a country walk. Veda wears an Edwardian dress, lace at collar and cuffs, many covered buttons running all down the bodice and skirt; George is in a silk tie and boater, marshaling a dapper cane. She looks shyly down and away, he is vigorous and direct, heading straight towards the camera. The third figure is Veda's youngest sister, Hilda. She is visiting them in Bradford, where they live. The year is 1913.

It is a warm day in the Yorkshire fields. Hilda's furled parasol speaks of intermittent sunshine. Veda's bag is light; perhaps a picnic has already been eaten. George cocks a cigarette between two fingers as he approaches the lens. The shutter speed must be very quick,

for there is no hint of a blur in their split-second motion; and what a mobile image it is too, so natural it looks as if this moment has been skimmed directly from life with something more sophisticated than a cheap Box Brownie. Two women, one man: the implication is that the photographer is Hilda's beau, and that this is a quartet on a double date. How large Hilda seems by comparison to Veda, who is thirty-three years old in this photograph—how large and how confident, looking enthusiastically back at her suitor, presumably none other than Captain Green. But I want to hold fast to my grandmother, the delicate feather in her hat, the fine chains of pale buttons—sixty that I can make out—which seem almost avant-garde, her gentle expression, the fascination of her unusual name.

George and Veda

The Elstons live in St. Paul's Road, Bradford. The house is a neat two-up two-down right next to St. Paul's Church, so close that only a small patch of green grass separates them from the door, aisle, and altar. George, also thirty-three, is the head of this little household. He is a commercial traveler selling lubricating oils to factories. Veda has been married to him for six years; they were late to marriage. Living with them is another of Veda's sisters, Daisy, younger by six years, who is working for the new National Telephone Company. She has a lively time of it, up and out every morning to connect one caller to another; but soon she will leave all this behind to join her husband, who is making a new life in India.

These facts emerge from the latest census. George signs himself George Maybrook Elston, always claiming to have been born in the month of May by a brook. My mother never quite believed in the brook, and it turns out that she was right. Only recently have I seen the narrow house in the industrial port of Hull where he was born in May 1880 into an atmosphere of death. Walter Elston had died very suddenly in February, on the stroke of his fortieth birthday, leaving his wife, Lauretta, a pregnant widow of thirty-four. She already had two sons to raise and was taking in lodgers even before George's birth. It pleases me, irrationally, unjustifiably, that her real name was Laura; it pleases me even more that she twirled it into the professional sobriquet Lauretta. For George's mother was a dancing teacher, who also gave music lessons to young ladies and gentlemen. Almost the only dragonfly memory we have ever been able to net from his unspoken past, however, is that her business came to a sudden end, and Lauretta was forced to leave Hull with her sons for a cottage a few miles away in the village of Kirk Ella.

Lauretta, bereaved, financially ruined, managed to keep going with a few local lessons. She finally moved to the nearby city of Selby, but then she too was gone, dead at forty-eight. George was an orphan at thirteen. I wonder who looked after him. Nobody, presumably; he was within a few months of leaving school and going to work. Perhaps his seventeen-year-old brother Fred was still at home, or maybe George just fended for himself.

Immediately I picture the toughness required, the instinct for self-preservation, the foreshortened youth and the damaging grief. But I cannot know exactly how far this altered him, whether this is how he came to be the difficult man he is said to have been. My mother knew nothing of George's early life and she never asked; it was unspoken in Chapel.

There are two stories, however—or facts that have been rounded into stories. Really they are just fragments, undisputed because there is nobody left to correct or confirm them. The first is that George sang in the choir at Selby Abbey. And why not? His mother taught music and dance, and he was later in a band. I can find no evidence, and neither could my mother when she once enquired at the Abbey. But it matters to me because it mattered to him: evensong in this soaring medieval church was something he was known to be proud of.

The second is that the small hall where Lauretta taught dancing burned to the ground one night while everyone was asleep. Any proof of this has vanished as completely as ash. But the fire would certainly explain her abrupt removal from Hull. I want to say that this was a disaster too far, that it ruined her, weakened her fatally after raising three children on her own while somehow keeping up the teaching all the way through. But there is no death certificate. She might have died of an accident, or marauding cancer.

And almost all I know about George's father is that his whole family life was contained in a single decade. At thirty he was a bachelor. By forty he had married Lauretta and conceived three sons, the last of whom he would never see in this life. Walter Elston was a color-maker in a Victorian factory, specializing in the new chemical paints. It delights me to think of this great-grandfather of mine—two strangers, now united in one possessive adjective—spending all day surrounded by hues: creating color.

But thus have I tucked him up, neat in my understanding, when his life can have been nothing like this simple summary. He walks through windy Hull to work in a factory; he is a boarder in various lodging houses all through his twenties; he marries a woman rather older than himself (either Lauretta or the official documents, which don't match, lie about her age). He may have been terminally sick for years, or he may have been felled by the sudden jamming of his heart. All I have is the proof of his last will and testament, to which Lauretta was executor, in which he falls into the common legal category of leaving less than three hundred pounds. Which may mean two hundred and ninety-nine, or one.

Lauretta had those two older sons, John and Fred. I have no idea where John goes, or what becomes of him beyond his youthful career as a draper's assistant in Scarborough, a fleeting detail from a census, after which he disappears. And so does Fred. George never saw either of them again. He seems to come from nowhere, solitary and *sui generis*, and so does my mother. Would it be so different with the advent of telephones and rapid transport? Possibly not— my husband has ten cousins he hasn't seen for decades; my father and his sister lived two miles apart in Edinburgh, but the occasions of meeting were only ever high days and holidays. His Glasgow uncle went away to New York and never returned. During the Second World War, my father was posted to America and tracked Uncle Bob down to the barbershop he ran in the Bronx. They talked for a brisk hour, all they could sustain.

And beside me in one of my own wedding photographs is a man

I have met only once, a distant cousin here to represent a column of dead relatives. I would not be certain of his name were it not on the back. In the great democracy of family albums we all have photographs upon which, disastrously, nothing is written. Identities drift in a sea of unknowing. We have no idea who they were, these people smiling, frowning, or resisting the camera's tyrannical hold. Each may be somebody, or nobody, of importance to the past or future story.

I have a picture of a despondent woman who might be Lauretta, in the usual rustling black silks of a Victorian widow. The card is stamped with the address of a studio near Hull. If it is her, then she certainly needed the gaiety of her assumed name. Lauretta sounds so modern, evocative of vaudeville or the American Wild West, although there is also one in Boccaccio's *Decameron*, published in English around this time. There is a certain raffishness in adopting this Italian-sounding name in 1880, as she did. This was the same year that Veda was born.

Nobody alive knows how George met Veda, daughter of the innkeeper at the Vine. Veda's father also died when she was young (her mother, no longer able to keep the job, brought up six children by letting out rooms in an old building on St. Leonard's Drive in Chapel). Her history surfaces only through marriage, alas, like so many women in those days. She was born in Hogsthorpe, but I do not know where she went to school, whether there were other suitors before George, why she was given this name Veda—pronounced to rhyme with *cedar*—with its strange Indian origin (I cannot find an actress, author, dancer, singer, or any other star after whom she could be named).

But I have something more precious, for I remember Veda myself. She came to live with my parents in Edinburgh sometime in the 1960s and was with us until I was five. So quiet, her blue eyes gentle, like everything about her. She used to hold a glass jar up to the sun for me to see its radiant cobalt-blue beams on the bedroom wall. When she died, I inherited both her room and the magical jar, which, when opened, turned out to hold the humble menthol scent of Vicks.

Veda had briefly been a governess in Leeds, only ten miles from Bradford. But she is otherwise sunk in an unlettered past. Not a single document survives; all that remains is her cookery book, containing fifty recipes for cakes based on exactly the same few meager ingredients, ingenious variations made from slightly different tinctures. She won every cake prize at the Chapel village show, concocting these delights entirely on a primitive paraffin stove.

The photograph of the country walk shows Veda as I can hardly imagine her but as she once was: a young wife, sociable, exquisitely dressed (more so than Hilda, I delightedly note), stepping out in the world. Images are all I have of the early Veda and George, these fragments of time held intact down the century in tiny sepia rectangles, so public and yet so intimate. Of course, there is something trapping about the shot, pinning us to a particular moment's veracity, suffusing our knowledge of a person or persons with this one circumstantial vision: this frozen instant. After all, my grandparents did not always go down that road, take those walks, dress up for such occasions. There was not always freedom or time; Hilda would not always be with them.

But there is another image, infinitely more valuable to me, showing a moment that did happen over and again, that kept occurring all through the years the Elstons lived in Bradford. It is a photograph of everyday truth—but what a picture.

Here is Veda in that neat little house, photographed by her husband in the first year of marriage. She stands stock-still in their modest kitchen. The exact size of this room is standard for its time and place—ten feet by eight. Their home is the end of the terrace. At the front of the building is the parlor, customarily shut up, partly because it would mean another fire to light and another room to dust, partly to preserve its status and decorum. The parlor gives straight onto the street through the front door. Behind it is this back room, which serves as scullery, kitchen, and living room all in one. A single water pipe runs diagonally down the wall to what

looks like a tap in the darkened corner. A kitchen cloth and another apron are tucked into it. Behind Veda is the stove, such as it is. Before her is the side window that looks onto the narrow passage separating the house from the churchyard.

This window is open. It is late spring or summer. Veda's dress is light cotton, striped, the sleeves rolled up. On the table before her is a small theater of objects: some bowls, a brown glazed teapot, and a rectangular pie dish. She is peeling apples for this pie, and the dish is the white enamel type that eventually chips, exposing a thumbnail of black tin. I have it still, as I have the teapot, which came from India; and I used to have the knife, so sharp it could skin a pepper, never mind an apple, lost to customs on my first flight abroad, foolishly unwitting that the blade could be considered dangerous. These objects connect both ends of a century.

The sunlight coming through the window is strong and clear, responsible for making everything visible in that room on that day, but also (literally) for creating this photograph. It is diffused through the rectangle of white muslin so that the image is evenly focused and lit. This is an unusual feat to begin with. Most family photographs at this time were taken outdoors, because the light is so much easier to handle. But not this one: George is fascinated by the sunlight and has thought hard how to use it in this cramped back room.

The radiance of his new bride is to be matched by the gracious light flowing through the window: that is the point, and the poetry of his picture. It is a beautiful image by any standard, carefully considered, exquisitely lit and composed. Almost a wedding gift from husband to wife. And they are both there together, united, breathing the same warm air.

The photograph implies the photographer.

George is not quite in the same room, though. To take his picture, he has opened the door that separates the parlor from the kitchen—there is the elliptical shape of the brass knob on the right—and positioned himself just over the threshold into the front room. The kitchen has three doors: this one, the one on the left that leads to the staircase, and the one at the back that gives onto the yard. George has opened one and shut two to arrange the light perfectly—or so he has to hope, for he has no certain idea how the picture will turn out until it returns from the printer. All he has is judgment and sight, and the natural light stealing through the Victorian window. But when the image is developed, it looks like a painting; specifically, it looks like a Vermeer.

Think of Vermeer's woman reading a letter in seventeenth-century Delft, or the painting of a milkmaid at a table illuminated by a side window, the filtered light bathing the figure in gentle purity: a condensed sonnet of absorption, solitude, and slow time. Veda stands in the same session of silent thought, three hundred years later. But my grandfather had never seen a Vermeer; he had never even heard of this Dutch artist who languished in obscurity for centuries after his death. Vermeer was still a minor obsession as late as 1912, when Proust has his character Swann plead an essay he is supposed to be writing on the revelation of Vermeer to get out of tea with Odette. And later in the sequence of novels, when the fictional writer Bergotte suffers his fatal heart attack while contemplating the famous patch of yellow wall in *View of Delft*, Proust still could not assume that any of his readers knew the painter's work. George had no access to art magazines, and no illustrated monographs on Vermeer had yet been published. None of his paintings were in British museums.

George is a traveling salesman who would like to have been an artist. I think of the technical drawings that won him that award of distinction as a soldier. The lives of even quite recent generations might almost disappear from our understanding if we did not think of their aspirations. He yearned to be something other than what he was, at a time before free education, when people had to make themselves up from what was available—the dance school, the local factory where his father had worked (and where George started out as an apprentice). Then came the Boer War in South Africa, robbing him of more youthful chances. Reality suppressed the dreams. He had to make money to look after Veda, to provide for the clothes she sewed, the apples she peeled, the children to come. His drawings are all gone to dust. But here, in this photograph, in this redemptive moment, George Elston is an artist.

And the picture was not made with an ordinary Box Brownie. The image measures 3 inches by 4¾; it does not fit any film format for the Brownie. There are various possibilities for the camera and processing method he might have used, but most likely is either a glass-plate camera, or a folding bellows camera with a roll of film. He sets it up on the back of a chair, perhaps, to keep its perfect steadiness (nothing is out of focus), a camera presumably borrowed, for there is scarcely another image from this time in his life, and George could hardly afford such equipment.

A photograph is a body of knowledge as an image but also as an object. How it was made tells so much. There they are together, man and wife, and the exposure time must be quite long, especially if transmitting light onto a glass plate. Almost impossible to imagine in our era of instantaneous images, this duration somehow makes the scene more poignant. They breathe; and they hold their breath.

Veda looks slightly down and away, diffidently self-conscious as she is in every photograph. I have the recipe she used for this apple pie in her handwritten book with its slow copperplate. It is not complex, just a bit of pastry and fruit. I have seen the pattern from which she made this shirtwaist suit, stitching the cloth by hand, the pleats on the sleeves surely her own flourish, like the many dozens of buttons on that dress in the picnic photograph. The picture is like a painting, but more than any painting it is shot through with the actual shadow of life—the momentary essence of Veda.

It is extraordinary to me that George and Veda can have had earlier lives in Hull, Selby, or Bradford, these chill northern cities. They exist to me entirely as figures rooted in a diminutive seaside landscape. But of course George is a rover, always on the move. He learns how to fix industrial boilers (exactly the same job as my other grandfather in Scotland, who progressed to superintendent of a Victorian swimming pool). From Hull to Selby, Yorkshire to South Africa, and two years at the front of the Boer War. And then somehow he meanders back to Bradford, presumably for work, where he meets Veda. And then he will go to Lincolnshire, and circulate around England for another thirty years until his retirement.

His suitcase: its appearance, long ago, used to make Betty cry because it heralded George's Monday departure. There is a curious moment in the birthday memoir where she writes of the week dragging slowly by, of waiting for his Friday return from her lookout upstairs: "There was a long view to the bend in the road along which he would at last appear, walking with heavy leather case. I would rush out to meet him, helping with five-year-old ardour to carry the suitcase. There might be a pencil box or purse or some other trinket from the utterly foreign shops away in the abroad of Nottingham or Bradford. I used to assist in the packing and unpacking of that case. It is sorrowful to think that my ready and willing pleasure in being an integral part of his affairs, and his in mine, not only came to an end but dramatically reversed."

Of George's traveling career I have only a dim shot of a Jack Russell outside a Macclesfield pub; my mother has no impressions beyond this age. Nor did she ask any questions. I can imagine the lonely life, trying to make a home of a rented room, reading newspapers in weak gaslight, eating with some fellow traveler in the station hotel, and then returning home as if the weekend was more real than the road—as if Chapel was his true existence. One day his daughter stops running up the road to greet him; after their schism, the Friday arrivals are as joyless for George, perhaps, as the Monday departures once were for Betty.

In the same year that George and Veda were born, 1880, the house where I grew up was built. It had a hidden staircase that led to a balcony between two narrow attics. You stood there beneath a cupola flooded with silvery Edinburgh light looking down through the stairwell, painted many times over by my father on scaffolding with long poles until he got it exactly the right yellow. I thought, and still think, these high places are the best in the world. Round lunette windows high above the boulevards of European cities, where someone is lucky enough to live; secret attics above department stores; narrow rooms perched on top of nineteenth-century brownstones in New York. Nobody need know you are there. I loved being up in the attic, reading, free, out of the way, my father painting in the studio below, my mother weaving her tapestries. Some of my dreams are still set in that house: running up the winding staircase, lying on the bed in the bare attic, seeing the green sea from its high window. I used to look across to the lights of Fife, spread out along the shore at dusk, and think it was like the French Riviera. The attic bred in me a taste for empty rooms. On that bed, where I slept, were the cotton sheets brought back from India by Captain Green.

Unlike her sisters Daisy and Hilda, Veda never traveled to India or anywhere else overseas. The farthest journey she ever made was the translation from Lincolnshire to Edinburgh to live with my parents in the 1960s. She never returned to Chapel, but somehow made a second life for herself in Scotland. I look at the photograph of her in the Bradford kitchen, seeing the same grace that was always there even in the deafness and frailty of age. She is no blood relation to me, but I wish I had inherited some of her traits, instead of the Indian teapot.

Perhaps it was Daisy's departure from their Bradford home to join her husband in India that sent Veda back home to Chapel St. Leonards and her mother, Rebecca. Perhaps she was lonely with George away all week. Of those two decades and more before Betty came to live with them there is very little news, except for a few details sieved from the local papers. Veda plays whist with some success for charity, wins various village competitions, sits loyally on the church council for many years (as does Miss Moore, not incidentally: she features in the leaked minutes, gossiping and complaining). George conducts a small band at fund-raising dances at the village hall or the Vine. He also plays the drums, his services required at festivities in surrounding towns and villages.

Apparently they go to fancy-dress dances in Chapel. One of Veda's costumes was Eat More Fruit—they had titles—and she was covered all over in pictures of fruit cut from magazines. Another was Mrs. Which-Way? in which she dressed back and front exactly the same, with two pairs of kid boots attached to her feet, pointing in different directions. They reveal a humor (although also a pathos, to me) that my mother never seems to have beheld in her parents. But she does recall the great celebrations for the Coronation of George VI in 1937.

George, ever one for dressing up, decorating, had glorified the front of our house with various emblems of the occasion—royalty, glorious Great Britain, flags winning first prize for his remarkable achievement. But no less theatrical was his creation for children set on a horse-drawn farm cart, suitably be-flagged. There am I the centre figure, as Britannia, helmet and shield just like the figure on the coins, sitting with trident raised, surrounded by every country in the empire, children wearing appropriate outfits for Canada, Australia etc. This talent of George's, which in another later age may well have taken off professionally into stage design or costume, was surely unique in a very un-lively village of potato growers.

But Veda was the most astonishing player that day. When the entire village was assembled on the green for the judging of best fancy-dress costume, first prize was awarded to someone who hadn't been there at all: Mrs. Veda Elston.

Everyone looked around, and then stepped forth a bedraggled old tramp. Gasps of astonishment. What came over that reticent, middle-aged respectable woman, to transform herself in old dirty clothes, head to toe, hair concealed under a bashed up old hat, who had spent the day sitting on the roadside with an old pram full of rubbish; she had even asked the local bobby to pretend to say move along, and most daring of all, had taken an empty beer bottle to the Vine, banged it on the counter and demanded in a gruff voice to have them "Fill it up mister!" Even I wasn't sure if it really was Veda.

Hilda, not long after the Bradford photograph, married Captain Green and had her two babies. All of Veda's sisters had families. But no children ever came for this unassuming woman, until her adopted daughter in 1929. By then Veda and George had been married for more than twenty years, during which the temperaments embodied in the walking photograph had become dramatically pronounced. Veda was increasingly self-effacing, peaceable, quiet; George's vigor had transformed into irritability. My mother remembers his frustration, days of rising anger followed by nights of bronchitic coughing. How could patient Veda stand it?

George descended from soldier to boiler mender, and then on down to salesman of textile lubricants and eventually soap. On commission, which dwindled dramatically as textile soap itself became a thing of the past. Church meetings at Chapel were full of anxiety about work and the Great Depression of the twenties, the parishioners fretting over the General Strike in 1926, the year my mother was born, and the terrible unemployment that followed. The Jarrow March passed close by through the Midlands; many Chapel villagers were out of work. That George hung on as long as he did seems miraculous now, for he kept working until my mother turned twenty-one, when he was sixty-six and in very poor health. Even from the start of his career, the commission was so slim that they had to make ends meet—or rather, Veda did—through summer lettings. For three years, she also took in Daisy's children.

Daisy had met and married one of Captain Green's friends from the Raj; indeed, she seems to have been the one who introduced Hilda to her future husband. But unlike Hilda, Daisy actually went out to live in India for many years, coming back and forth to Lincolnshire to leave each of her three sons in Veda's care as they became old enough to go to school. They boarded with the Elstons at weekends and during all the school holidays, three lads aged between eight and fourteen. This was all well before my mother's time, and how much she wished it hadn't been. "I used to spend long hours with their photographs, making believe that I had three brothers. I knew their faces so well and was faintly jealous of these happy boys playing on the beach with my so much younger mother. She always seemed so terribly old to me. They wore school uniforms of gray with black and white ties, attending Orient College in Skegness—it only now occurs to me that this bizarre name was not so inappropriate, the school being filled with the left-behind children of Raj families."

At last came a day when these mythical cousins and their mother materialized. "The emotional sequences of the event were so typical of many a later occasion—high expectation and unrestrained excitement beforehand, instant repressed abashment when the visitors appeared, tongue-tied blushings and all sorts of agonies that made the whole thing unbearable and a matter for reactionary sobbing and disappointment afterwards. For the three boys were now grown men, and the eldest, David, was even going thin on top though I fell romantically for the young Pat, a pink-gold-blue paragon in his early twenties."

To my horror, among those old Lincolnshire newspapers I recently came across a trial centering on this supposedly happy and convenient boarding arrangement. Veda is forced to sue her own brother-in-law for failing to pay the agreed fees. All this time she has been looking after the three boys, and even when Daisy and her husband have returned from India to live in Harrogate, they still fail to cough up this long-delayed sum, until the judge decrees it.

What anguish and anxiety this must have caused the Elstons. And perhaps George's harsh treatment of the eldest boy—he once sent him to bed for failing to return from the village shop with the right brand of cigarette—takes on a slightly different complexion. The intense stress and anxiety of having these three large boys in the small house, and of entertaining them during holidays, and keeping them fed and clothed and their schoolwork done, and all the while the money from the soap commission running out and no fees coming from India. No wonder it would later take Daisy so long to pay a visit.

Why were there no children for Veda herself before Betty arrived in her life? As a young woman she had undergone a fairly serious operation, always a secret spoken of in hushed whispers, sometimes, curiously enough, in the changing rooms of dress shops, where she seemed to find it necessary to confide in the assistants because of a slightly enlarged waistline. She never would wear skirts, the way some people won't wear trousers, only dresses. My mother was allowed to know, many years later, that she had suffered an ovarian cyst, and the worst thing about the operation for her was a great thirst that came after the anesthetic. "Veda was nil by mouth. But she begged piteously for a drink, and the Irish nurse at last gave in to the plea for forbidden liquid, threatening to 'knock her bloody head off' if she disclosed the incident to Matron. The relish with which she repeated the oath was comic, as never in her life did she use 'language' of this coarseness herself."

Was it an ovarian cyst, or a botched hysterectomy? Whatever it was, Veda's infertility was undisclosed—*unexplained*, in contemporary parlance. Much later, exactly the same thing would happen to my mother, strangely; she had to wait for her children for many years until her condition was acknowledged and eventually cured by a very simple method. She has never ceased in her gratitude to the surgeon, saying that her life began anew. Later still, the same thing happened to me.

Someone once sent me a postcard, for morale, of the *Madonna del Parto* by Piero della Francesca, a painting my mother also loved as an art student on a traveling scholarship to Italy. It shows two angels drawing back the curtains of a tentlike pavilion to reveal a Madonna with eyes gently lowered: a column of calmness, beautiful in blue. We had always thought the Madonna was pregnant—she has one hand to her waist as if easing the weight, and the other just below her breast where a seam in her overdress has been unstitched, as if her clothes were growing too tight. But looking at this postcard, I suddenly wondered whether she was not pregnant at all, just gesturing at a mystical future she could only imagine. This crisis of faith came because I had just believed—hoped—that I was safely pregnant again, after the loss of a baby. I could not look at paintings of pregnant women at that time without wondering whether they really were conclusively with child.

We need images, quite apart from anything else, when we have no words. The postcard was an encouragement from a friend who couldn't have guessed how bad the timing would be. But how is an artist to represent fertility when it is an unknown quantity, invisible until the body shows it? And its opposite: infertility? I can hardly summon even one image to mind. Barren land, seeds cast on stony ground, the empty vessel—biblical metaphors, all, that speak irrefutably for themselves without need of illustration. Perhaps one should not be surprised that fertility clinics have no idea what to put on their walls. Something as vague and inoffensive as a computer-generated waterfall; I suppose they don't want to raise your hopes. But it is in these clinics that some of us may see the first, best, most astonishing images of new life—in my case, two sequins of light twinkling on the dark scanner: my twin daughters' beating hearts.

And how does that feel? I don't have words; as so often, an image is better: specifically a painting made by a monk in a cell several centuries ago. A woman is receiving the news that she has conceived; an angel tells her so. In fact, the split second of the telling is, in a sense, the conception. Mary leans forward, hands crossed over her body as if receiving a blessing, but also protecting a new life. Her face is a graceful portrait of that singular moment between universal awe and the dawning of more bewildering emotion. It is Fra Angelico's *Annunciation*—sudden revelation made visible.

8

The Post Office

War came to the Lincolnshire coast. Soldiers unfurled vast coils of barbed wire along the beaches to protect vulnerable villages from the much-threatened German invasion. Air-raid shelters were hollowed out of the ground, and tank blockades began to appear in the landscape, abrupt as boxes dropped from the sky. In Skegness, Browning machine guns stood ready to strafe the Luftwaffe from angled mounts in the fairy dell, where children had lately paddled in the blue-bottomed pool. Butlin's was transformed into a naval base.

Billy Butlin was a shrewd entrepreneur, ever-zealous to expand his empire. Just before the outbreak of war, he had shipped a whole amusement park out to the International Exhibition in Liège. Four hundred tons of roller coasters, merry-go-rounds, shooting galleries, and bumper cars now had to be transported back home in haste. He hired Belgian boatmen to load these outlandish contraptions onto barges, dragging iron horses and ghost trains through the country's slow maze of canals in the darkness of night. Ships ferried them the last few miles across the Channel to Hull, in May 1940, just days before the Nazis invaded Belgium and British troops began the agonizing evacuation of Dunkirk.

The fair equipment was eventually stowed away in farm outbuildings in Ireland, and Butlin lent all his holiday camps to the Admiralty as part of the war effort. The camp at Skegness was transformed into HMS *Royal Arthur*, as if it were itself a ship. The bright colors were painted over, the dance hall became an armory, and air-raid shelters were concealed beneath the jaunty flower beds. The surrealist painter George Melly, stationed there as a petty officer, remembered that the navy could not quite suppress the atmosphere of gaiety. The main office was still covered in murals of brilliant-blue seaside skies, and officers had their meals in a faux-Elizabethan inn called Ye Olde Pigge and Whistle.

Lincolnshire, with so much flat shore on the east coast, opposite Belgium and the Netherlands, was strategically ideal as an embarkation point for British ships, and also as a launching pad for bombing raids. It is known to this day as Bomber County. Centers for training pilots and soldiers sprang up around Chapel and Ingold-mells, and the whole area took on the character of an armed encampment, a sinister inversion of Butlin's, with added barbed wire.

My mother was thirteen when the news of war came into the Elston household, funneled through the wireless in the kitchen. This was controlled, of course, by George, who censored the worst reports in favor of Churchill's great morale-boosting orations. It all began with Neville Chamberlain's broadcast on 3 September 1939 announcing that the Germans had been asked to withdraw their troops from Poland by 11 a.m. that day: "I have to tell you now that no such undertaking has been received." It is a curious fact that nobody ever remembers the declaration of war, only Chamberlain's grave intimation to the British people at 11:15.

George switched the radio off and instantly set about making blackouts for the windows.

Our neighbour Mr. Simpson was a joiner with a big store room of plywood quickly available, and my father measured and cut with rapid accuracy. It looked bleak indeed, until curtains covered up these wooden panels. The ritual of putting up the blackout every evening was strictly followed. In a small village, the air raid wardens on their bicycle circuits were acute discoverers of any forbidden gleam of light.

George immediately put himself forward as a soldier, this time joining the Home Guard, dressed once more in wartime khaki at the age of fifty-nine. A sergeant in the Boer War, he had been promoted from second lieutenant to captain in the West Riding Volunteer Regiment during the Great War—a position that, incidentally, put him on equal footing with his brother-in-law, Captain Green—and now used his considerable experience to teach signaling to local farmers, veterans, and other men who were not called up. They practiced semaphore in the potato fields, tapped out Morse messages through the telegraph wires at the post office on Sundays, remained ever-ready for invasion. And their role was not without danger. The Luftwaffe attacked Butlin's four hundred times in the first three years of the war; unexploded bombs are even now being found on Chapel beach.

I have crossed those fields where George paraded with his troops, the low-lying earth still yielding up its victory crops. The wires are all still in place; the path from the Elstons' house to the church in one direction, and to the post office in the other, remain unaltered. The dun, green, and gray palette is no different. And yet I find it almost impossible to believe that George and I walked the same landscape, felt the same emotions, had the same joy in the enormous sunrises that radiate over Lincolnshire, noticed the same gull-flocking dusks, loved—if he did—the same Betty. He is as remote to me as some soldier in the *Anglo-Saxon Chronicle* we translated at university, unreal, incomprehensible, a figure trudging through the plowed fields of an illuminated manuscript. It is not just that I never met him; it is that my mother has made of him an absolute stranger.

In 1940, all the local road and street signs were removed so that German parachute troops falling to earth around Chapel would have no idea where they were. A prisoner-of-war camp was set up less than a mile outside the village, and hundreds of wireless operators were employed at Butlin's, all ready to trigger the firing of torpedoes at any slight hint of an enemy submarine. Everyone in Chapel lived in fear of an imminent German invasion, which might arrive this very day on this very beach on this very stretch of the English coast. After all, leaked news of Operation Sea Lion revealed that Hitler was preparing to gun down the English on their very shores.

But my mother remembers none of this. Perhaps George's home guarding protected her from such knowledge. What she does recall is the peculiar fact that she was allowed to visit the coastguard's lookout, up the long wooden stairs to this frail hut perched on the sandhills in the path of the North Sea gales, where old Mr. Andrews, the burly coastguard, peered through his brass telescope for ominous vessels on the horizon. Somehow Betty was permitted to go with him, for a brief period at the outset of the war, as if his lookout was the safest place on earth. But it was not long before household fears curtailed her freedom.

I can't forget the night when the invasion was most imminent. Leonard Short, also Home Guard, had received a message to raise George, who dressed and rushed out. We were quite uninformed as to where, why, what. But this was full alert. The adults must have been terrified. I remember the tapping at the window and all of us sleeping downstairs in case of this dire news and the urgent voice of Leonard calling Mr. Elston to get up, get up, get up! I went to school next day as if nothing had ever happened.

At Skegness Grammar, Headmaster Spendlove issued all his pupils gas masks, which they found hilarious, running round the assembly hall laughing at these goggling gadgets. Perhaps it was one of his last cheerful moments as a teacher. In December that year, boys between sixteen and eighteen were required to register for national training. A month later, all eighteen-year-olds were conscripted.

At school was a handsome lad named George Allenby, hero of the field and an academic scholar. He signed up at seventeen as a pilot and was swiftly flying sweeps across the water to France. On return, he used to drop notes from the cockpit down to school friends on the playing fields below and perform victory rolls above his mother's house. All this spirit, all this gallant levity, ceased one still evening in May 1940 when his plane crashed into the sea eight miles from the shore. I have seen a photograph of Allenby, captain of the rugby team, strong arms folded, head tilted as he squints at the lens in the Lincolnshire sun. How rapidly was this schoolboy trained, flying perilous missions, and then dead, before his eighteenth birthday. Mr. Spendlove wept as he announced the death of Sergeant George Allenby to rows of bewildered pupils in the assembly hall. Later, he seems to have suffered a kind of depression at the loss of so many of his boys.

In the autumn of that same year, a dogfight took place at twilight over the shallow waters of Chapel Sands. A Heinkel was seen in the gathering darkness, attacking an RAF Hudson bomber, which spun back with all guns blazing. The crew of the Heinkel managed to jump out of the cockpit and into the sea only moments before it crashed. Amazed villagers saw two exhausted Germans struggling through the water to collapse on the dim shore. One was a boy of eighteen, the other a veteran of forty, both with Iron Crosses and freely admitting that they were glad to be alive and out of danger. They were immediately interned in the POW camp.

*　*　*

The beach is a stage, washed new each day in the half-light of dawn. The village is an audience to every performance, the sea an ever-changing backdrop. And so it always has been, long before the Saxons came to pick edible seaweed, or the Romans channeled their elaborate drains into the tide, or medieval villagers took their walnut-shell boats out on the waters to fish for a living. Here is where the tall ships stalled and smugglers plundered cargo by night; where beacons were lit during the Napoleonic Wars; where men and women courted down the centuries in long dark clothes and striped Edwardian bathing suits and T-shirts and bikinis; and where generations of children built their first sandcastles. Messages in the sand, pebbles spelling out significant names, keys and rings disastrously lost: the everyday theater of the shore. Early racing cars hurtled up and down in the Roaring Twenties. The *Hindenburg* sailed overhead, imponderably slow, in 1936. Here is where the Caprons supposedly sent clandestine signals to the enemy, where a Second World War colonel was arrested for treason, where dogfights took place and incendiary bombs fell. Ninety years of picnics and summer holidays have come and gone since my mother's kidnap, as if it too had never happened. Each day's events are wiped clean by the tide.

The sea covers almost three-quarters of the earth's surface, but few artists before the age of flight ever imagined its immense geographic spread across the globe. Leonardo, as so often, is the pioneer. Around 1515, he made a watercolor known as *Bird's Eye View of Sea Coast* in which he imagines the sea off Italy, snug to the curving bays, meeting the land like a fitted blue carpet. The image is partly a map and partly a relief, for the land is wavy with mountains. But mainly it is a vision of how the sea-covered world might look from way up in the air, where the war pilots fly.

On a clear day the sea at Chapel is like a Seurat, crystal clear in its frozen shimmer of sand–sea colors. On a breezy day it is a Turner, the waves meeting the sky in a rolling vortex of liquid and air, the two elements blending in one of his rapid watercolors. "Pictures of nothing, and very like," was Hazlitt's barbed remark; which, turned on its head by modern critics, makes Turner a pioneer of abstract painting. And what is the sea but a perfect abstraction? The sweep of sand stretches away in that blurry miasma of motion, color, and light that Turner captured so miraculously in a thousand paintings. He could be right there at work on Chapel Sands, I sometimes think: the sea remote and withdrawn, a distant bar of blue far away across the strand.

Unlike so many other English artists, who cannot resist bathers, parasols, or paddling children, Turner's beaches are empty.

Which is how Chapel would have looked in his day. In the first half of the nineteenth century, the beach was solitary, too far from the nearest railway station to be a popular bathing spot. It carried certain dangers, for the placid tide sometimes lost its temper in momentous gales that overwhelmed the undefended village. The Elizabethan historian Holinshed recorded in his *Chronicles* that the whole of Chapel was lost in 1571 except for a paltry few houses: "A ship was marooned on a housetop, the church was washed down except the steeple and a Master Pelham had a hundred sheep drowned."

Even when Victorian tents began to appear, and then beach huts, and a small wooden café, the tide would rise up and wash them away. The first guesthouse on the sea bank was extraordinary for its daring: patrons could open the front door and step straight out onto the sand. But the owners abandoned it after constant battles with the sea, and emigrated to Australia. The deserted building gradually crumbled, until the floods of 1922 swept it clean away.

Visitors, on period postcards, constantly remark that this is all there is on this particular stretch of the Lincolnshire coast: nothing but sea and air. But it never feels that way to me. I look for traces of my mother's story here; for what is sand but the pulverized past, ancient history in billions of particles? Something of her—of all these people—must still be here, or so I want to believe. But of course the tide never stays still, and the sands are shaped by it, endlessly shifting, restlessly dispersing out across the wide world.

* * *

In the strange conditions of wartime, George Elston made a terrible decision. He removed his daughter from school without notice or explanation and installed her in the village post office. She was sixteen, and only a year away from qualifying for higher education. All her promise was now wasted in an even more circumscribed jail.

It was the darkest place of my life. Eighteen months in a very small Civil Service prison. My sentence was to be junior assistant to the Postmaster in a cubicle he had partitioned off from his real business as the village shopkeeper. At the far end of his large and homely grocery was my hole, a shoe box standing on end, not a chink of daylight, a naked bulb dangling from a dusty flex above my miserable head. Everything apart from the wooden till, which had to be balanced every night, was of paper, yellowing and ancient; old calendars, old telegram forms, leaflets about pensions and savings stamps—things that did not Turn Over rapidly, but gave a half-shuffle forwards every decade. The only mint-new things, brightly coloured by contrast—flaring red and Reckitt's blue—were the stamps, halfpenny and penny. Decrepit cloth-bound books fell open to reveal other sort of stamps which I had never known existed—insurance stamps of various kinds in faded greys and brown colours and the most perplexing values for the innumerate. "Five thirteen and three halfpenny agriculturals please," was the sort of demand which sent me into a quiver, and with stubs of pencils and backs of old forms I would try to cost it out, while some gnarled old ploughman waited suspiciously for the result.

George Stow, the postmaster-grocer, had grown to look very like his bacons and hams. Hams were suspended on hooks from a high wooden beam. He wore an ocher holland overall and sometimes a trilby hat, rarely removing his pipe while cutting cheese from a hunk that seemed to my mother the size of a small haystack.

He presided over every aspect of Chapel life from behind the long counter of the large shop, formerly the lifeboat house, which was in a sense his council chamber; for Stow was central to all decision-making, being chairman of the parish council and the vestry committee, vicar's warden and postmaster general of my mother's corner of the stores. He judged the vegetable competitions, occasionally won by George; he sold the bacon and eggs cooked by Veda, which were now strictly rationed. One or two other old men would come and lean over the counter through the day to turn over important village business, and some people actually came to him for advice. His store is still there today, now an omni-purpose bazaar, and Mr. Stow's name lives on, fifty years after his death, in the sign above the kiosk selling buckets and spades outside.

Among Stow's conversants was George himself. A photograph shows them together in a Home Guard group on the beach. I assume their acquaintance was what got my mother this much-loathed job. Perhaps Mr. Stow was trying to help by providing his friend's daughter with government work, for these jobs were pro-tected during the Second World War. She would not have to become a land girl doing farmwork or a Wren, leaving home to join the forces. But nor was she allowed to go to university. One day she was at school; the next she was standing stupefied behind a counter with a set of brass letter-scales trying to accept the crazy notion of handling government revenue, her childhood done.

The Till was to be the lord and master of my existence, the feared despot, the Serpent in the Garden of Eden. Its contents were to be a constant dread, to be counted each evening and made to tally with the in-goings and outgoings. For such an insignificant little wooden drawer to hold such power to make me capable of such suffering. For there was no going home, no release, until the wretched thing came right. And those aged rule-books cluttering up the shelves, held no answers for a deficit problem.

Occasionally old Mrs. Stow would appear with tea and a slice of cake to cheer my teenage mother onwards with her task. She even tried to help with these sad sums once or twice. I know this because I remember her as a figure from my own childhood, in the form of the tales my mother told. She is to me the kindly Samaritan who tries to feed the prisoner a morsel through the bars. The cake must be seed cake: that is my fantasy, and Mrs. Stow will be wearing a long white apron. Sometimes she is too busy to come; sometimes she forgets, and the hours trudge on, uninterrupted even by the cup of tepid tea.

As a small child, my mother had loved Stow's Stores.

Coming in to the warmth, to the mixed aroma of coke fumes and smoked bacon, on a bitter winter's afternoon, was a welcome moment. Near Christmas time especially, there were rare treats like snips of candied peel—halves of orange and lemon encrusted with a thick crystalline sugar—and raisins and currants passed down to small customers in a tobacco-smelling hand, while the adults congregated around the stove, chatting. Groceries were carried home in a flat straw bag called a bass being also the name of a fish, not one that we ever ate though, cod and haddock being the only two at Canning's fish shop.

Now her father had passed her on to this establishment without a word, without any thought of her future or her freedom, like an indentured servant. I can easily imagine the strength of his protective instincts, but to her it was just more tyranny and pathological possessiveness.

Veda came into her own during the Second World War, starting a canteen at the Elstons' end of the village where soldiers could be sustained with more than just tea. She helped to billet exhausted troops stumbling up the Lincolnshire beaches from action across the Channel or in the sea itself. Dazed figures sometimes appeared out of nowhere, and came to the house for comfort. Veda gathered around her a group of knitters, making socks for the troops rescued during the evacuation of Dunkirk. The wool was oiled and durable. I know this because my mother knitted a cardigan with the ends, oatmeal-colored with a brilliant flash of orange at the mandarin collar and single amber button. She wore it for thirty years, and I wore it long after her as a student, just as I inherited her golden mohair coat and moss-green corduroy jacket. I wore all the clothes she made for herself with such pride, loving their longevity and invention. My mother never looked like anyone else, and her originality meant that I didn't either.

Soldiers came to the post office to send telegrams announcing that they were safe and well. Betty might have had a walk or two with one of them. But the dark obverse was the kind of telegram received at her end, over the telephone. "I had never used a phone in my life till then, and have never quite got over the magic. It took precedence over everything that was happening, and the drama of receiving dictated telegrams through that old-fashioned daffodil receiver gave me a God-like feeling as to people's lives, with messages of life and death going through my hands." The mercy was that she only had to write down the devastating news; its delivery to those as yet unknowing parents was the fate of a poor bicycling messenger boy.

When I worked at the village post office one of the stolen fruits which was most reprehensible was the reading of postcards. One should never have done it of course, but confined all day every day 8.30 until 6 in a dark little box with no windows, small wonder I looked for companionship. Let into the wall was a tiny door, like a safe, which I would unlock twice a day to retrieve the mail which had been posted on the outside of that wall into a red letter box. This had all the thrill of searching for hens eggs in haystacks and barns, another huge childhood pleasure. Open the letter box, and what might be there today? Two or three envelopes, five postcards or—

nothing at all, depending on the season of the year. The post-card era in those days was very lively and in the summer time that box would be quite full of wish you were here coloured cards, stout ladies sitting squashed into deck chairs being attacked by crabs and lobsters. Each passage of writing set out to be my enthralment, above all in the unmistakably superior cards from the Misses Williamson, two spinster ladies who arrived every season to occupy their mysterious large stone house, shut up and shuttered all winter, among the sands at the far end of the village. What they wrote about I recognised as lively prose of a high order—the revelation of making gold out of straw.

The Misses Williamson inspired in her the gift of transforming the everyday that has enriched my whole life.

The stores where she sat are only a few yards from the beach. To put your nose outside the shop door was to inhale the briny air. But for six days a week, she never went outside, and even the news per-colating through the shop, in conversation, correspondence, and postcards, did not quite tell her what was actually happening, his-torically, in the war.

Ships ran aground at Chapel, sometimes badly damaged and even sinking. Two dead bodies had to be brought ashore in a crab boat in the near-dark of a January afternoon. When it became obvious that Germany would invade Norway, the Norwegian king took exile at nearby Ingoldmells, presumably thought to be the last place an assassin would look for him. A boy from Skegness post office was sent to him with an urgent telegram, receiving the kingly sum of sixpence from the royal purse. When the next telegram arrived, he made the mistake of handing it to an aide, who offered no tip. Henceforth the boy insisted that all telegrams were so urgent and so private they could only be delivered in person to His Majesty.

In Skegness, the promenades and car parks were used as drill grounds, the seafront hotels as RAF billets. For several years sirens wailed out at night, the all-clear not sounded sometimes until next day. Bombs dropped on the golf course and the cattle market, on cafés and campgrounds, and the Tower Cinema during a matinee. Strafing hit the church hall and a platform of Skegness railway station. People eating lunch in Miss Blanchard's café beneath the pier saw bombs hit the sands, then waited in horror for an explosion that never came.

At Butlin's, there was much amusement in that park of amusements when Lord Haw-Haw used his propaganda broadcast to announce that HMS *Royal Arthur* had been successfully sunk by the Luftwaffe. And then, quite suddenly, the enemy ceased to trouble itself with Lincolnshire and the whole direction of fire shifted to the great cities of the Midlands. Skegness beach even reopened in 1943, in the lull after the German action. And through it all, my mother never saw a man die or a bomb drop or even an actual German. She carried on knitting and sitting in the daily misery of the post office, six days a week, going home to a tea of margarined toast and mutton. Although every now and again the Elstons' diet was improved by the anonymous gift of a ham, left on their doorstep overnight and strictly against rationing rules. It turned out that they were given by a tall, bearded farmer named Joe Kirk. He was said to have had a liking for Veda. This puts something else in the scales, and pleases me very much.

It was here in the post office that my mother's love of Tennyson began, as she read in her dark corner between the infrequent customers.

On either side the river lie
Long fields of barley and of rye,
That clothe the wold and meet the sky;
And through the field the road runs by,
To many-tower'd Camelot.

She taught "The Lady of Shalott" to me and then again to my daughters before any of us could even read. The wolds of her childhood are there in this very poem; and Tennyson seemed to take his rolling rhythms from the local sea. He returned again and again to the stretch of beach that runs from Skegness to Chapel and Mablethorpe, where the Tennysons leased a beach house in summer. An early poem, variously titled "Lines" or "Mablethorpe," pictures that sea in an anti-postcard season.

And here again I come, and only find
The drain-cut levels of the marshy lea—
Gray sand banks, and pale sunsets—dreary wind,
Dim shores, dense rains, and heavy-clouded sea.
[. . .]
I love the place that I have loved before,
I love the rolling cloud, the flying rain,
The brown sea lapsing back with sullen roar
To travel leagues before he comes again,
The misty desert of the houseless shore,
The phantom circle of the moaning main.

When we first went to visit the new Great Court of the British Museum in 2000, my mother wept at the exalted light, the high fine world of the entrance hall, and above all the quotation from Tennyson set in the floor. She was so proud that it was by her poet.

Let thy feet millenniums hence
Be set in midst of knowledge.

"As a child every Sunday I walked along those long flat sands of
Tennyson's reluctantly," she recalled, "chided by the ever-blowing
easterly winds. In many poems there are lines which surely must be
drawn from his brooking along the miles at the sea's edge. The melancholy is so pervasive and in me too, in recollected grey skies and
dark seas. This is where my grandmother saw him striding out."

And it was from a piece of driftwood found on that beach that a
small box was carved, and given to Betty as a child. We have it still,
and it fascinates me, this art out of flotsam. Inscribed on its rounded
lid is a beautiful wish: *May your life be one glad song.* Who made it?
She cannot recall, thought it might have been someone staying in
the house. A holiday guest? Or Uncle Percy? Who on earth was
Uncle Percy? They were all so unconnected.

My mother is full of remorse that she might not properly have
appreciated the box as a child. Fancy someone wandering about
carving pieces of wood, she says; would anyone do that now? It is a
period piece, so perfectly of its era with post-Deco panels. And
whoever made the box perhaps also made the phrase, for I cannot
find it anywhere in literature.

As a child, I naturally believed that this box had in fact been carved by Tennyson himself, right there and then on Chapel Sands.

Looking for news of Chapel in the 1940s, I came across the war-time diaries of a villager named May Hill, later published by her children to commemorate their clearly brave and loving mother. Among the talk of air raids and rationing, of picking brambles and trying to shoot a wild rabbit to fill the pot, there is to my amazement a sudden appearance by my mother. She delivers a telegram in August 1943, when the messenger boy is off duty, and is later besieged by the sudden arrival of the British North Africa Force, returning from long and dangerous duty: "They were sending telegrams to let their people know they were home safe. A lot of them tried out their new French on Betty Elston. Expect they were a bit surprised at first when she answered their French inquiries. Mrs. Stow eventually came to the rescue." Earlier that year, Mrs. Hill writes: "Poor Betty has suddenly been taken out of school and is at Stow's post office at present. She is clever so probably won't be there long." Alas, she was wrong.

Like Isaac Newton, like Captain Smith and Sir John Franklin, yearning for the open water and an end to the flatlands, Tennyson did not stay. Dreaming of freedom, they all left, out to sea—or up into the universe, like the astronaut Michael Foale, a modern hero for Lincolnshire when he stepped out into space to repair a damaged spacecraft in 1999. My mother pictured him as another child on Lincolnshire beach, staring up into the high skies with visions of escape.

In the summer of 1944, an art teacher at Skegness Grammar who had noticed Betty's gifts, then lamented her unexplained departure, persuaded George to let his daughter return to the town for evening classes. Evidently flattered, he grudgingly let her go. She would draw through the evening, stay the night with the teacher, and then be back at the post office the next morning. This continued for many months until my mother got her freedom.

I wonder now who saw her reading behind the counter, selling stamps to farmers, trying to balance the hated ledger. She sat there for more than nine hours a day for almost two years, a young girl contained behind glass, framed in a dingy corner. Did the woman on the bus see her? The invisible grandmother? Were they shocked when she suddenly vanished?

A tutor from Nottingham College of Art somehow came across Betty's work and drove all the way to Chapel to convince the Elstons to let her apply. She was finally allowed to do so in 1946. She left her parents, by now in their sixties, escaped Chapel for Nottingham, and at long last began to live. Taught by this same tutor, she flew as a student, far away to Scotland, in fact, with a scholarship to study at Edinburgh College of Art. Here she became an artist, met my father, and married. Her life altered because of the vision and persistence of that one woman, Thea Downing. My daughter Thea is named after her, in memory and utmost gratitude.

One evening in the spring of 2017, my mother and I talk about our travels together. She can remember Lake Garda and the perfect lawn leading down to the water; she cannot remember going to Madrid or Vienna; she has no recollection of Ghent or—to my sorrow—France on the many occasions that we went there. But if I bring out a photograph, something returns. She can remember the night classes at Skegness, and being sent for the test at Nottingham College of Art, where she was required simply to paint orange and yellow wallflowers for two hours, at the end of which a Mr. Foster casually gave her an entrance pass without remark. She remembers being encouraged to apply for the Edinburgh scholarship by Thea and, on receiving the news that she had won it, running all the way from Mrs. Smith's digs right across Nottingham to tell her beloved tutor. We get as far as the move to Edinburgh and where she first lived—Frederick Street—and then, she says, rather suddenly and sadly, that it all fades out. What happens next is no longer quite within grasp.

And something similar happens with the birthday memoir. My mother wrote it again and again with slightly different variations over the next twenty years, always at my begging, in the hope that she might have more to say about the incidents of her early life, and their effect upon her. But she never got further than the post office, not even as far as the flight from Chapel.

When she left, it was to return less and less until she never came back at all. There are no photographs in the album of Betty during her student years—nor as a teenager—except one last shot aged twenty-three, home from a postgraduate painting scholarship in Florence. I know that George wept when she departed for Italy, for she says so in a letter to an old friend, part of a lifetime's correspondence recently bequeathed to me at this woman's death. Yet there is no mention of her own feelings towards him, or of the home she left behind, beyond those expressed in the memoir. Over the years, his bronchitis eventually declined into prolonged bouts of pneumonia. There were unexplained medical dilemmas. The news from home got worse, and in the freezing February of 1952, George Elston died. But still Betty did not go back. This most generous and ever-loving woman, so empathetic and compassionate, was not there for George's death and did not return for his funeral. I do not think she knows where he is buried.

9

Icarus

The first image my mother ever owned, as a new student heady with freedom and hard-won post office shillings, was Brueghel's *Landscape with the Fall of Icarus*. It was only a plate detached from an art book. But in those days such reproductions, which were printed separately and glued in by hand, might be so large and perfectly made that an old-master volume was like a miniature museum for those who would never see the originals. My mother took a scalpel and carefully filleted the plate from the page—they were tactfully attached by one edge only, as if asking to be pried free—and mounted the *Fall of Icarus* on cardboard. Later, we had many images in our house this way, from Fra Angelico's *Annunciation* to Piero della Francesca's diptych of the Duke and Duchess of

Urbino, he with his shattered nose jutting like a ledge, she with her complicated Catherine wheel of ribboned hair, a dream of misty hills between them. I first saw Dutch landscapes and images by Degas and Manet through liberated plates like these, and have always loved Manet's portrait of Zola sitting at his desk with a large book on one knee, the wall behind him dense with black-and-white reproductions of works by Velázquez, Japanese watercolors, and indeed Manet's own *Olympia*, the painter giving his tacit blessing to the humble prints that anyone—even great writers—might tack up.

The Brueghel was in color, golden with the last glow of that setting sun on the blue horizon, far away across a shimmering green sea. This immense expanse of light, flooding from near to far, gives an almost cosmological character to the painting, illuminating the curve of the turning earth and sending shadows into the field's ridged furrows, so sharp they look as if they could be plucked like the strings of some outlandish instrument. The soil is hard, parched, and brown, but spring's greenness infuses the landscape, sheep are beginning to find something to eat, and a partridge settles fatly on a bough. No other painting has ever made me feel so keenly alive to the idea that this high round world, lit by the sun, is the very same place where our ancestors once trudged and plowed and fished the very same seas, in their queer medieval costumes; that we may change but the scenery does not.

For no matter how strange those shoes, with their clodhopping toes; no matter how odd the pleats of the plowman's tunic or the plump knickerbockers of the shepherd staring gormlessly up at the heavens, this is a world we know (at least as far as the stately galleons), a northern landscape through which you or I might clamber even now. An airy globe where the seasons come and go, and a horse's backside looks just the same across half a thousand years; this timelessness will turn out to be part of the picture's highly original narrative. The scene ought to look as medieval as the workers who appear within it, like characters on a stage, and yet it never looks half as archaic as certain black-and-white photographs taken just a century ago.

The Brueghel moved from Nottingham to Edinburgh, where my mother eventually had the plate framed. It would be my first picture too, in a way; or at least, the first I ever saw, other than my father's paintings.

James and Betty met at Edinburgh College of Art after the war, in which he had flown as a pilot. Demobbed, and desperate to get back to the easel, he still wore his RAF uniform to classes, as servicemen often did in those straitened times. Instead of the traditional demob suit awarded to each man returning from the hostilities, my father had used his voucher to have a local tailor work with yards of wool cloth bought in Calcutta during the war.

But what had looked a rich tawny brown in the dark heat of an Indian shop proved nearer to pink in the cold Scottish light. Better the uniform than the embarrassment.

James first went to the college as a sixteen-year-old, before the outbreak of war. I want to call him the prodigy he was. My mother revered him for his intellect and draftsmanship, but he seems not to have sensed it while they were students. A first attempt to woo this beautiful chestnut-haired girl from England went badly awry. Seeing her in the distance, coming towards him down the long corridor by the sculpture court, he mustered the clumsiest form of words. He could get her a ticket, he said, to the annual college revel, where students dressed up in fantastical costumes (often as artists: my father had such Spanish looks he naturally transformed into Velázquez). My mother replied that she was quite capable of getting one for herself. It was another year before they spoke again, twelve long and wasted months. But this time another kind of accident brought them together. My father had locked himself out of his attic studio in a building on George Street (today a boulevard of restaurants and boutiques no student could possibly afford) and tried to climb back in through a skylight. He fell, broke his ankle in three places, and ended up in the Royal Infirmary. By now they were both postgraduate teachers at the college, and almost the only young people in the staffroom. My mother felt obliged to visit my father in hospital. It was here that they fell in love.

The lives of our parents before we were born are surely the first great mystery. For me their stories are backlit with a silver-screen radiance: my father and mother painting from dawn to last light, sometimes meeting only at midnight; attempting the dangerously steep rock upon which Edinburgh Castle stands—illegal, indeed the police were waiting at the top—and driving through snow-storms in an unheated car to London to see tapestries from Egypt and paintings by Cézanne. My father teaches life classes, among his models the old man who once posed for Eros in Piccadilly and the

teenage Sean Connery, then an Edinburgh milkman. I know about my father's incessant drawing and his selling of a portrait—the only conventional likeness he ever painted—to pay for dinner with Betty at the city's expensive French restaurant. I know about their deep love of work. Here is my father fairly attacking the canvas, always driven onwards, no time to rest his mind (or cigarette); here is my mother at the sink where the students cleaned their brushes on the wall above in an ever-growing carapace of paint. He teaches night school five days a week; she walks miles to meet him from her digs. On Mondays they go to the Cameo Cinema to see *Les Enfants du Paradis*, Orson Welles's *Othello*, and Marlon Brando in *A Streetcar Named Desire*. My father has a record player but no money for records. "Twist and Shout" is the only disc I remember from childhood.

In 1953, they marry. He is thirty (a one-woman man, who seems to have been waiting for Betty all his life); she is twenty-six. After living and working together in a series of studios, they move into the Victorian house down by the waters of the Firth of Forth where I grew up. My father had the main bedroom to paint in; out of a chaos of empty cigarette packets and old grocery boxes, paint-encrusted saucers and palettes, oil colors hardening as they oozed from the body of crushed tubes, the radio wrapped in polythene to save it from spatters, he made works of extraordinary serenity and

perfection. I loved the smell of turps and oil paint that stole out from beneath his door and crave the faintest hint of it still, like an addict; it takes me back to him, and the one solace that he was lucky enough to be able to work as he did, abstract and semi-abstract paintings, day into night and even next morning, right up to his early death of cancer.

My mother no longer painted after she was married. She used to say that there was only room for one painter; but I hope that it was because the warmth of wool drew her to weaving, and the soft warp and weft of tapestry. She worked in another bedroom, her loom a large iron rectangle like an empty picture frame that slowly filled up with images in wool. When I was a child, she wove fire trees and winter landscapes, scenes from poems—Malory and Tennyson—songs and fables. I remember the princess and the pea, the emperor's new clothes with a puny pink hominid at the center of a gaping crowd, and a marvelous kaleidoscope of changing patterns and colors that might have been the rose window in some medieval cathedral. She wove the landscape of the Scottish Borders by the light of a sickle moon, a vision of misty hills, sheep, and a secret rabbit haloed in its hole; a partridge sits plump in an oak.

My parents had hundreds of images in the house—photographs scissored from newspapers, reproductions pinned to walls, postcards from distant galleries sent by their friends. Growing up I collected these in a shoebox, beginning with the cave paintings of Lascaux and ending, I seem to think, with Seurat's *A Sunday on La Grande Jatte*, sent by an American student of my father's all the way from Chicago. But the Brueghel was special, sacred, a world both light and dark and mesmerizing; plainly a narrative that any child could follow, and yet powerfully strange, even to adults.

It hung in the hall, and then in the kitchen, and eventually in the small cottage in the Scottish Borders where my parents later went to live. We looked at it by night and by day; by chance and on purpose; on the way to and from school, over meals, on our way upstairs to bed. In the cottage, it hung directly above the old table shoved against the damp wall in the kitchen where we could stare at it while eating Heinz tomato soup and Marmite on toast.

We see pictures in time and place, and in the context of our own lives; we cannot see them otherwise. So even though I know this painting evokes the first song of spring, it speaks of deep winter to me, partly because of the sepulchral gloom of that nearly window-less cottage by the Tweed. Its furrowed darkness somehow had an affinity with the brown soil of the dank December fields and the grain and dust of Borders farms; and our hut of a cottage seemed completely of that era too, practically medieval to us children. Yet the plowman's pleats are stiff as a modern gymslip and his queer headgear resembles a motorbike helmet; the dog's no different than any dog today, nor the sheep, nor the birds. And for me it spoke, and still speaks, of the enticing thrill of theaters as well as the countryside. Brueghel puts us up in the gods, in the balcony with the plowman, while the play goes on far below in the breeze-riffled waters. There is seating farther down in the stalls, where a man fishes the waves without noticing this drama. But nobody bothers with him.

Landscape with the Fall of Icarus was an object as well as an image, and I was aware of the mildew on the mount and the thickness of the paper on which a printer, far away in the Flanders from which this painting originally came, had laid down these rich and perfect tones. As a small child I did not realize that it was a reproduction; it had the same status for me as the pictures in books: small worlds into which one looked, as into a doll's house or poem. Surely they were all unique? And this picture of Icarus felt right for its size, the little legs disappearing into the sea like tiny joke limbs, as if this were one of Aesop's fables rather than a solemn Greek tragedy. I did not know that there was an original painting in Brussels; that it was much larger and only comparatively recently discovered when my mother extracted its reproduction from the book. Or that people might one day say that this was a version of a lost original. I didn't know where it hung or that it was painted in oils. It was a picture, not a painting; a scene, a story, a vision, not a panel worked in pigment. You could take it off the wall and stare down into it, discovering the lone black sheep and the strange decapitated face in the trees through a magnifying glass.

This picture hangs in my London home now, where my daughters do not notice—as Brueghel surely intended, with his extraordinary pictorial ingenuity, slowing down the action as he slows down the eye—those flailing legs plunging into the water. The fall of a miniature Icarus. The figure is so small as to be immediately overlooked, dwarfed by the prominent rump of the horse. Indeed, most visitors looking at the painting in the Musée des Beaux Arts, which gave W. H. Auden's famous Brueghel poem its title, miss the tragedy at first; which is the point of both poem and picture.

There is no real foreground and background here. Every part of this painting speaks to the next. Icarus drowns in the same sea that men fish for a living—the very men you are looking at. The pale yellow sun that radiates across the high sky and the wide waters, the force that melts the wax of his wings, that fells him, punishing his hubris, is also what makes everything visible. Everything is happening at once; everything is connected.

The plowman plows his magnificently sharp furrow, echoed in his own gymslip pleats. He might be turning the brown soil of any lowlands landscape, Lincolnshire, Flanders, the Borders. Trading vessels sail on across the sea, forging on with their business. The sun casts an extraordinary aura over the indifferent world and life continues, just as death and disaster occur unheeded. The villagers simply go on.

All of my mother's images have something of Brueghel about them; she even painted a series of seasons, and of children's games, just as he did. She sees the world in fables and festivities, and in its full beauty; her humor rises up, evergreen, despite the formative anguish. Auden emphasizes pain in his poem about the picture—torture, martyrdom, sudden death, the scenes of horror painted by the old masters, how they take place "while someone else is eating or opening a window or just walking dully along." But there is infinite beauty in Brueghel's scene, and even something undeniably comedic about the plowman's pudding-bowl helmet, the shepherd who is still looking dumbly up at the sky long after the fall, and even in the silly tumbling legs. William Carlos Williams's great American poem about the picture comes much closer to my mother's celebratory view of life, which loves the seasons and the sunshine.

According to Brueghel
when Icarus fell
it was spring

a farmer was ploughing
his field
the whole pageantry

of the year was
awake tingling
near

the edge of the sea
concerned
with itself

sweating in the sun
that melted
the wings' wax

unsignificantly
off the coast
there was

a splash quite unnoticed
this was
Icarus drowning

Brueghel's masterpiece makes me think of the way my mother does not quite notice disaster, or at least does not take it in as others might: not the war, the dogfight over Chapel, or the fallen boy-soldiers. She looks the other way, at the springtime, not the splash. In her late eighties, never having been ill before, she suffered a heart attack. All the way through the urgent journey across the winter countryside to hospital, through the operation and beyond, she kept her eyes closed so that the last sights she saw would not be the nameless wires and contraptions swinging around inside the ambulance, or the faces of strangers in the hospital glare, but inner visions of her own life and family. She flees death, attends no funerals, does not countenance annihilation. The hollow cake.

And perhaps it all begins with the claustrophobic silence of home, the sense of abandonment that came with George's weekly departures and Veda's retreat to the kitchen, and then Betty's longing to escape the sepulchral gloom of this walled-up childhood. Home is where nobody ever says anything by way of explanation about loss, death, or tragedy; where it is possible for George and Veda to explain nothing about anything, for a whole childhood to pass, with all its racing school weeks and Sunday longueurs, its endless summer holidays and cyclical autumns, without anyone ever telling her anything—for the secret of her own origins to be kept entirely from her. The catastrophe is happening and everyone is looking away. Everyone, except the grandmother who desperately wanted to see her.

Nobody notices the legs the first time. Nobody sees much beyond the plowman at the front of the image, and the vast span of sunshine receding all the way back to its source. We might never connect the sun with the legs at all, if we didn't look harder, look closer, search the image for all of its content. Icarus flew too close to the heat; the sun's rays melted the wax of his wings and he died. The current title of the painting, *Landscape with the Fall of Icarus*, gets it about right. (Titles are a comparatively modern invention, and susceptible to change.) First there is the enchanting landscape, and then there is the legendary fall. Except that it has already happened. Look closer still, and you may see the hint of a hand thrashing above the waves; Icarus has fallen into the sea and is now fighting for his life. But the green sea is closing over.

Images hold the world before us, unwavering, unchanging, fixed before our eyes. But we may look again, and again, seeing and understanding more. The focus shifts, the relationships change, the meaning deepens every time.

My mother discovered the truth about who her father really was by looking at an image; looking and seeing almost by chance. At some point in her teenage years, she began to examine what her adoptive parents had told her; or perhaps she began to question their authority. At the same time she had a growing sense of her own appearance, and a great wondering about where she originally came from, whose face might have an echo in her own. One day an official photograph was required for some now-forgotten purpose. She took the bus to a professional studio in Skegness. The shot was taken and the result posted to Chapel. My mother looked at her picture and saw George.

The proportions, the length of the face, the shared cast of the features: all were graphically condensed in grayscale. A mechanical object, with its indifferent eye, had confirmed the truth. Miniaturized and distilled in black and white, on this stiff little card, Betty sees herself as others see her; and the photograph says she is his.

What she did next has baffled me. For my mother simply contained the knowledge. She did not rush to tell—or accuse— George, not that day or any other, even though he had lied to her over and again. First Betty grew up believing that George and Veda were her birth parents. Then he told her that she was adopted. And then he allowed her to go on believing this for years without revealing that she was his natural daughter. But perhaps my mother got her own back in the end for she never told him what she knew, or that she had learned who he really was through the pure and simple evidence of her eyes.

Betty would come home from the grammar school, and then the post office, to sit silently opposite her father at dinner. Perhaps the new knowledge was another barrier against him, her innocence reinforced by his guilt. In this moment she determines to be as unlike him as possible; and perhaps we really can will it. For somehow she managed to give me the happiest of childhoods without any pattern or example, having experienced nothing like it herself.

How did George think he could fly so high above her? How did he ever believe he could keep the truth of his paternity from his own daughter? He seemed to think that this belated story of her adoption, this poor picture of events, would suffice. Did it never occur to him that his clever child might sense the connection between them, observe the similarity, guess at the truth, and that she might then wonder how on earth she had come into being? And that when she knew, there must come an additional realization that George had betrayed poor Veda as well; that there must be another mother somewhere else. Perhaps she might even suspect that this tale of adoption had been concocted as a fiction or cover-up behind which Veda—and, of course, George himself—could carry on living their respectable lives in the village of Chapel St. Leonards.

The world goes on. The skies, now short of Icarus and his prodigious folly, arch above us while great or tiny incidents topple us below. The Chinese poet wonders whether this can be the same sky, and the same moon, as the one he saw all those years ago before he was exiled. I cannot quite believe that George walked the same earth, that we are related, that I share his blood, so remote is he through silence and estrangement. But Brueghel's painting helps me to know it is so. Here we all are by the sea again. Our forebears move through the same landscape, and it is not a monochrome world.

I wonder now whether George actually believed he had achieved it, sustained this arrogant and foolhardy deception all the way from my mother's birth in 1926 to his own death in 1952. He certainly did not manage to deceive his neighbors. But it turns out that he had arranged the official fiction very carefully, through lawyers.

Since my mother never told him what she knew, it is quite possible that he went to his death believing she had no idea. Which may have been a self-wrought agony, I suppose, along with her final alienation from him. Betty left for another life and George lost the child he had fought so hard to possess. Did he reap what he sowed?

10

The Agreement

With the birth of her children in the 1960s, my mother began to wonder again about her own origins. She had no clues about her early life, no anecdotes, letters, or pictures of herself before the age of three. She had never seen her own birth certificate. This document had to exist, of course, although George had been unable to produce it when requested by Headmaster Spendlove. In 1966, she decided to return to Lincolnshire, taking a room at the Vine, where Veda was raised, where George took his drinks, where she herself had worked as a holiday waitress, to search for evidence of her past.

And what news there was. In a solicitor's office in the market town of Spilsby, the registrar reached up to an orderly shelf of 1920s files and efficiently retrieved her certificate. On reading it he became embarrassed. It was his reluctant duty to inform her that there was no mention of a father, only a mother; that she was, *ipso facto*, illegitimate.

This she had realized long ago; what she did not know was where and to whom she was born.

Her birth is recorded as having taken place on 8 August 1926 at the High Mill in Hogsthorpe. She is called Grace. Her mother is Hilda Blanchard, twenty-one years of age. The only other family member cited in the document is Fred Blanchard, father of Hilda, and proprietor of the windmill and bakery. Grace is the baker's granddaughter.

The baby has no middle name, but she does have an enigmatic initial. It lies there, singular and unexplained on the heavy paper. She is registered as Grace E. Blanchard.

My mother was forty when she saw this document for the first time. She had already passed from Betty Elston to Elizabeth Cumming on marriage to my father, but now she had another new identity to absorb and intimations of an earlier life before the one she knew. She had come into the world at a mill, perhaps to the sound of turning sails and the grinding of grain, perhaps to the scent of baking cakes and bread, in a village stupefyingly close to Chapel. Her birth mother was not long out of childhood herself. And this young woman had given her a better name, so much more beautiful than unmusical Betty. Grace: a syllable of what might have been.

My mother had not known that she was once called Grace. She had never asked Veda about her early life, given the secrecy and suppression of the Elston household, and had only now consulted her because she needed the exact name to find the certificate. Veda gave the details, and more. "In 1966 I approached Frearsons solicitors to ask if any documents still existed relating to my birth or adoption," my mother wrote on the envelope that still contains the papers, "and they replied in the affirmative, but would not let me look at these unless written Authority was received from my adoptive parent still surviving. This Veda Maud Mary Elston gave." One may imagine the tact and regret involved in appealing to Veda, who was then eighty-six years old, frail and deaf and half a lifetime away from George's betrayal, each woman anguished to think there was a first mother.

Veda knew precisely where the birth certificate was and what it contained because she had herself stood in this very office in Spilsby nearly four decades earlier. For Frearsons had one further document pertaining to my mother, and this was the adoption agreement by which Grace was handed from one family to another, changing name as she went. The signatories are Hilda Blanchard, George and Veda Elston. Every harsh word of it indicates that it was drawn up as an immediate response to the kidnap from Chapel beach.

The agreement, in red and black ink on thick parchment, is dated 14 November 1929. A cold Thursday in a grave year of hung parliaments, poverty, and global depression. In the wide world around them, Italian teachers are forced to join the Fascist Party. Stalin exiles Trotsky. The Wall Street Crash is at its absolute lowest. But there is nothing in the world as important, on this day, to these people, as the signing of the document.

Hilda is called The Parent. George is titled Commercial Traveller. Grace is the child they are passing between them. The terms are brutal and binding. The Adopters shall have "the controlled custody" of the child until she is twenty-one. She shall bear the name Elston and "be held out to the World and in all respects treated as if she were in fact the child of the Adopters." And here comes the first catch. Hilda must never do anything to undermine this fiction. In order to bring Grace to regard herself as the Adopters' own child, "the Parent shall not herself, nor shall any other person on her behalf or with her consent hold any further communication with the Infant or attempt to convey to her any information as to her actual parentage or attempt to remove the Infant from the care and custody of the Adopters." What happened on the beach that day must never happen again. That is the implication. Hilda has tried to take her daughter back from George, claiming her off the sands at Chapel; and the Elstons have resorted to a lawyer. There must be no further connection, no future plots to kidnap Grace, who now becomes Betty in the stroke of this tract, no more attempts "to speak to her, or to interfere with the control, education or management of the Infant."

And of course there would not be—as far as the Elstons knew— for another decade, until that day on the green country bus.

Now the document becomes threatening, and needlessly cruel. "The Parent shall not institute any legal proceedings for the recovery of the Infant." She must rein herself in, let the child go, never try to contest this binding document—a document quite possibly made up out of George's own head. For it is by no means a standard contract. And if the Parent should ever attempt to breach this deal in any way, she must "forthwith repay to the Adopters the entire amount expended by the latter in the maintenance, education and support of the child as ascertained debt." An unimaginable threat to a young woman with no funds to speak of. And then comes the reward, such as it is: that if Hilda Blanchard abides by all of the above terms, then the Adopters will finance the child "for the cost of her maintenance and education."

And they agree to it all, this strange trio. Hilda Blanchard signs in the presence of the Hogsthorpe blacksmith, Mr. Janney, father of a childhood friend, who has perhaps taken the day off to travel to Spilsby and act as her witness. She gives nothing but her initial and surname. But there it is: her signature. This was the first time my mother had ever set eyes on Hilda's shapely handwriting. George spells out his full name, as always, and is witnessed by the manager of the Victory Hotel in Leicester. Poor Veda has no witness except Miss Moore, secretary to the very solicitor who is drawing up this document; the same Miss Moore who sat next to the woman on the bus. No wonder she remembered it all so well later.

It is impossible to say who signed first, what order these signatures took. But the fact that George was in Leicester, the document presumably posted or carried there with him, indicates that they were probably never in the same room together. What a mercy for all involved—for Veda, so betrayed, now agreeing to accept into her life the child of her husband's infidelity; for Hilda, forced to give up her daughter under pain of incalculable penalty; and for George, who would have had to look them both in the eye on this day of reckoning.

How strange that the agreement should pivot on money, that the leverage—and the threat—is financial. George will come after Hilda for untold sums if she ever tries to speak to her daughter, or sue for her return. The model, one senses, may have been the court case between the Elstons and the Johnstons, where Veda had looked after her three nephews for years without receiving the promised payments. Except that this time the minor concerned is George's own daughter. The housing of children equals the spending of money: a Dickensian contract, fit for Scrooge. Or is there another way to see it? George is so desperate to have possession of his daughter, sole offspring, child of his heart, that he unleashes the one substantial threat he can come up with: take her away from me again and you will pay back every penny.

The Adoption Act had only recently been passed in 1926. The whole possibility of surreptitiously commandeering someone else's child was now over, at least in theory. Before the Act, children of all ages could be "borrowed" in perpetuity, brought up by sisters, neighbors, aunts and uncles, or even just random strangers who took a fancy to some child whose parents could not afford, or were not able, to look after them, or who simply believed that the child might have a better life elsewhere. Children from orphanages were distributed this way, or handed in to orphanages in the first place because their mothers had too little money or too many other children. Infants grew up believing that their aunts or grandmothers were their mothers; whole villages and communities conspired to keep the exact truth of an unwanted teenage pregnancy from the growing child. Notorious maternity homes passed babies straight on to adoptive parents, taking fees from both sides, and children were often shipped overseas without any background checks, particularly to countries such as the Netherlands, where adoption was frowned on by the government. In a bid to stop the casual disappearance of children from orphanages overnight, specifically, progressive legislators in the House of Lords pioneered a new Act to protect both children and their birth parents, most usually the mothers from whom these children were effectively stolen.

An Adoption Register was established in 1926, and every case was to be recorded in detail. The names of the birth parents must be registered, and so must the name and address of the adopter. This of course meant that it was possible for the adopted child to trace the birth mother in later life. It also meant that the child could trace the father, if the parent's name was known. If my mother had consulted the Adoption Register, she would have discovered not only the identity of her birth mother, Hilda, but also the fact that George was her father.

Except that there was no such entry.

My mother had in fact started her search with the Adoption Register. She traveled from Edinburgh to London by train to consult the archives, and found no trace of her case; which is why, with considerable reluctance, in case it distressed her, she was forced to ask Veda.

It turns out that George evaded the law. He never legally adopted my mother at all. I only know this because I live in the Internet age; my mother was searching on foot, as it were, and the long trudge through the woods did not give her the aerial picture of today. For George to adopt his daughter with full legality, in 1929, would have meant giving away the true relationship between her birth parents, as well as putting Hilda Blanchard's name on public record. So the document they signed that day is nothing more than a business deal, a collection of terms upon which they somehow came to agreement. Which is perhaps where the money comes in. George could hardly take Hilda to court if she tried to retrieve her own child, for he had not legally adopted her; but the contract meant he could come after her money.

It might be argued that he had no need to adopt his daughter at all, since he was her "natural" father. But in establishing this arrangement, he also managed to erase his own paternity from the record (nor did it appear on the birth certificate) by drawing up the document himself. Did he do so to cover his own secret, to conceal it from his daughter, to protect Veda, or Hilda, or for all these reasons? It is doubtful whether the adoption agreement could ever have been binding in any case, whether it was worth the proverbial parchment upon which it is written. But this is part of the tragedy. Did Hilda, or Veda, for one moment suspect this?

A more unfathomable complication of my mother's early life is something almost accidentally implied in the agreement, namely that she seems to have been back and forth between two lives. This child who has been Grace Blanchard in one village is now Betty Elston in another. For three years she has been living with her mother at the mill in Hogsthorpe, and now she is to live permanently with the Elstons at Chapel. But only if Hilda does not try to "hold any further communication with the Infant . . . or attempt to remove the Infant from the care and custody of the Adopters." The warning is very specific, the possibility as real as if it had happened already. Grace is at the mill, then the house in Chapel, then she is stolen from the beach, perhaps taken back to the mill later. A sense of to and fro is inscribed in the document, which was signed less than three weeks after the kidnap.

My mother knew nothing of this incident in 1966. We only learned of it twenty years later. To her, the agreement seemed a testament of longing and despair: a very young woman deprived of her child, forced to hand her over to bullying George, who has paid a solicitor to come up with terms so menacing as to keep Hilda well away. According to the Spilsby solicitor, the contract officially "extinguished" all Hilda's rights as a parent, although it could hardly have killed her feelings.

About these, my mother must have felt keenly herself, and yet she has never spoken of them to me. Perhaps she guards herself against the anguish. The document was painful enough, a revelation of chaos and casual bargaining with a child. It increased the retrospective sadness of her youth; whereas for me, growing up, it was the spar of hope for which I continually reached. Hilda must have loved Grace to have fought for her this way; George must have loved her to have fought back: this was what the document signified. And all those childhood imprisonments—never allowed out of the garden, no playing with other children, withdrawal from school to the post office jail—perhaps they were extreme methods devised by George to protect Betty from "attempts to convey her actual parentage," or to snatch her back again from the Elstons. The direct breach of the adoption contract by the woman on the bus, whoever she was, trying so hard to bring Grace back to her grandmother: this was another proof of love. Against all this runs the certain knowledge that Hilda actually agreed to this intimidating contract and handed over her daughter for reasons as yet unknown but which might be guessed. Still, I could even make the intimidation a measure of feeling. What was George so afraid of: another kidnap from Chapel Sands, or the power of Hilda's love for her child?

My mother knew Hogsthorpe well, had cycled through it a thousand times as a girl. She also knew the Blanchard name, with its French origins and overtones of Thomas Hardy. It would have been

perfectly possible for her to travel straight from Spilsby to Hogsthorpe—only twelve miles distant—the very morning she saw Hilda's name on the birth certificate, or to have walked up the short
road that evening from the Vine Hotel to the bakery. She might
have discovered the identity of the woman on the bus, who always
got off at Hogsthorpe; she might have searched for the grandmother
who wanted to see her; she might have tried to find her birth
mother. The map was, after all, tiny. But she was always fearful of
hurting others. Had she gone any further, it might have brought
maelstrom into Hilda's life, and grief into Veda's final years, for she
was already suffering from heart failure and soon to die. Here is the
dilemma for the adopted child: how to love and respect both mothers, the one unknown as well as the one who is here every day. I
suppose my mother was trying to honor both. But all the possibilities were sidestepped, and slipped away.

These people who invented us—who were they? In my own case, I
have no doubt. For my mother, the identification was impossible.
She really had no idea about any of them, even after seeing the documents in Spilsby. Recently, driving with her in the car, I asked
about her parents, whether Veda was an anxious woman, given all
she endured. "If she was, she never showed it." And George? "I have
no idea. I do not know either of them." She speaks of them in the

present tense, and suddenly they are with us in this instant: two people, once living, once lived with for almost twenty years, yet forever unknown.

When Veda died in 1967 and my mother had to visit another lawyer to read the will, she found her origins invoked once again. Veda left everything "to my adopted daughter Betty." The phrase must have been a legal requirement, but it communicated a lingering sense of detachment, as if the ruthless document still held sway.

The effect of this visit to the Spilsby solicitor was to make my mother cease searching, at least for the moment. She wanted the truth, the sense of identity that comes from knowing about one's birth, to add to the experience of living. But precisely what had she learned? Hilda's name, her tender age, her proximity to Chapel; very little so far. But there was one immediate and jolting realization, and it concerned a childhood puzzle. In Chapel each day arrived that regular baker's van from Hogsthorpe, cream-colored, with BLANCHARD painted in capital letters on the side. Out of it got Harold Blanchard, the baker's son, calling with bread for the Simpsons next door, then the Robinsons, and so on—but never for the Elstons. A strange anomaly of Betty's youth was now suddenly and sharply explained.

II

George and Hilda

Is it tactless to put their names together? Who knows anything profound about their union except that they produced a child? The only thing that can be said about George and Hilda for certain, at this stage, is what the document deliberately avoids: that they met—once, twice, many times?—and then came to an agreement never to meet again, while passing between them a daughter.

My mother went no further than this after her visit to Spilsby. Friends advised her not to pursue this girl who had given her up; who would not or could not keep her; to whom she once belonged, in her words, but who then disowned her. Hilda might not want to see her again; only consider the distress of a second rejection. For the next two decades, all my mother had of Hilda Blanchard were her name and signature. And one more thing: a pair of dates, telling her that Hilda was twenty-one when Grace was born, and twenty-four when she agreed to the adoption, which left three unaccountable years.

We have since learned that Hilda Blanchard was born in 1904 to Fred and Mary Jane, who ran the High Mill and bakery at Hogsthorpe. She was one of five children. Her brothers were Frank, Arthur, Harold, and Hugh, such classic Edwardian names. Frank was three years older; Arthur was younger by five years. There are traces of him in public documents. At the age of fifteen Arthur was apprenticed to Gamages department store at London's Holborn Circus, famous for its toys and model railways. At the age of sixteen, he was carried off by appendicitis. This desperate death occurred only weeks after Grace's birth. In the space of two months, the Blanchards gained a grandchild and lost a son.

Hilda could not have been more than twenty, and was perhaps even younger, when she first met George Elston, then in his forties. A May–December romance is common enough, but how could she possibly have been drawn to the George I had heard about, bad-tempered, suspicious, morose, and dictatorial? All the tales of him ran counter to any kind of romantic affair, and the tenor of the adoption agreement implied aggression. Hilda was surely the victim of George's force. An encounter, a grappling, perhaps not even preceded by a flirtation: it can only be imagined, and yet it must not be imagined. To cry rape is to offend Veda's memory, to horrify my mother, to subject an unknown grandfather to summary justice when he cannot speak for himself. Just to think of the moment of your own mother's conception is unnatural in any case. We should recoil at this taboo.

The only time we ever talked of it, my mother thought it might have been a more Hardyesque seduction. A courtship, a young woman overwhelmed, a pregnancy that could barely be acknowledged. Only twenty when this fate befell her, Hilda's heroism lay in her endurance. She could so easily have been one of those fallen women from nineteenth-century French art, throwing herself into the Seine by night with stones in her pockets, dredged from the foggy waters at dawn, face still lovely in death. Instead, Hilda Blanchard carried the child, gave her life. And then could not bear to part with her; was pressured over and again into handing Grace over to George, with his threats and his legal documents. Four years after they first met, he is somehow still in her life. For the encounter must have taken place in 1925, given the August birth. A toss-of-the-dice moment that produces the accidental child: How on earth could they have met? At the Vine, a village dance, on Chapel Sands? Or is it something to do with the windmill, Fred Blanchard's bakery dispensing bread round the neighborhood?

From Chapel to Hogsthorpe is a mile or two along a lane scented with limes, its flatness sporadically interrupted by windmills scalloping the sky. You could walk in thirty minutes from the beach directly past George's house and on up the road until Chapel melts into Hogsthorpe with its medieval church. The crow's flight takes you rapidly from the sands to the mill, from George to Hilda.

Hogsthorpe in the 1920s numbered not quite five hundred people, including half a dozen smallholders and twenty-three farmers. What marked it out was a surprising range of shops—a butcher, a baker, not one but two shoemakers, a pair of blacksmiths (including Mr. Janney, witness to the adoption), a confectioner, three separate grocers, a bricklayer, plumber, and wheelwright. You could have your hair cut in Hogsthorpe, have bicycles and baskets custom-made and later repaired, order your coal, and employ the services of a doctor. The elementary school had room for more than a hundred pupils, including a succession of Blanchards—Frank, then Hilda, then Arthur, Harold, and Hugh. Three of these souls lie in the graveyard now, outside the church they attended as children, where they were christened and confirmed—and where my mother was christened as well. When she is born, this new girl child must be carried up the long main street to the church for the ceremony, perhaps to the various shops, to Sunday services where Fred sings in the choir, in and out of the post office which is connected to the one in Stow's Stores; my mother and Betty Janney, the black-smith's daughter, will one day be in constant touch over telegrams. Betty Janney knows all about Betty Elston.

So does Reverend Drake, who has held the Hogsthorpe living for twenty years and christens the unexpected infant in his church. She appears in the register as Grace Ellston [*sic*] Blanchard, the initial ful-filled as a name. So does Dr. Paterson, for it is he who delivers my mother. (As he will one day sign George's death certificate.) So do the butcher, the baker, and all. And good Fred Blanchard, who buys his grain from the farmers, sells flour to the grocer and the confectioner, delivers the daily bread to all the surrounding villages: he is on speak-ing terms with all these people. He must realize that they know.

A postcard of the Blanchard windmill exists from around 1911. It soars high and black, a tapering brick tower, tarred to keep out the slightest breath of damp that might steal in through the air and ruin the dry grain. Capped with an onion-shaped ogee, it has four great fantail sails that catch the wind and turn the flywheel several storeys below, connected top to bottom by pulley. Fred Blanchard had no engine until the late 1920s, and could not mill the wheat and corn without that wind. But on a day of high breezes, he and his employees could turn out four tons of flour a day.

Hauling on the brakes, lugging the sacks to the perpetual sound of grindstones loud enough to drown out a voice, the men are always encouraging the mill to go a little faster, to make a little more flour. One of the sons, Frank Blanchard, was said to have climbed up and hung on the sails, wheeling round in the air for fun; while inside the mill, these same sails drove the centrifugal drills, the revolving stones and shifting sieves. And all these millers, in their Edwardian shirtsleeves, appear in the photograph taken that day a century and more ago. Here is Mary Jane Blanchard in the doorway in leg-of-mutton sleeves, two of her children perched on the wall. The boy is this very Frank; the little girl in the hat is Hilda, my grandmother. Except that this pronoun is like a stile I cannot get over. The connection between us was diverted, as if a dike had been thrown in the way. She is my grandmother, and I am her granddaughter, but I can only reunite us with words, the joining of people through writing.

Here they stand like chess pieces stationed upon a board: a family and the staff who have become a second family. The postcard shows a hardworking group, clearly united, all day together at the mill. The house is so close, separated only by a drystone wall, that everyone must have been in and out all day, with Mary Jane a kind of mother to them all. The grain arrives by cart and leaves in the form of finely sifted flour, silky as hair, or in batches of cottage loaves, round Lincolnshire rolls, and trays of fresh jam tarts.

And immediately I picture my mother there, through the front door that opens straight into the big kitchen. She is being held up to the table, on a stool or, God willing, somebody's knee, excitedly holding the spoon she has been allowed to dip in the strawberry jam. Slowly, carefully, she fills the tarts. Grace is the smallest child, an infant niece to the boy uncles, one of whom is only eight years older. She is the daughter of the baker's daughter.

And this is what she had—all she had—from those first three years: this strange free-floating memory of jam. No photographs, no letters or other recollections. I remember that she was once envious of Fred Astaire, who also had no memory of his first three years of poverty in Nebraska, except for the ceaseless shunting back and forth of the freight trains near his house. He had the sliding thrum of those engines as a sound and rhythm running all through his tap-dancing life, whereas she had not a single memory of that mother, those grandparents or uncles, not the vaguest ghost of a person or place, only the spooning of jam.

Public records give me a little more of Hilda, who attends Hogsthorpe school until she is eleven and is then admitted to Louth Grammar as a weekly boarder. Another clever child, she too excels in English. Every Monday she travels to the grammar school, returning home on Saturdays, back to the windmill and the chores. Like my mother, Hilda leaves school with no obvious route to the university she would certainly now have attended and is apparently taking up nursing work at the time of Grace's birth. The certificate describes her as a mental health nurse. Does disappointment set in already, at twenty: a life limited to Hogsthorpe and Louth? George Elston, older, wiser, traveling around Britain, playing in a dance band, known for his sharpness, whichever way it cut—might he have seemed alluringly worldly?

Hilda's mother Mary Jane was one of fourteen children from a family of lime burners, her father Joseph illiterate. Her headstone in the graveyard, now gone, testified that she was much loved. A photograph in an amateur history of Hogsthorpe shows a neat and tiny woman, shining hair and round spectacles, standing by her moustachioed husband in a perfect scene of solidarity outside the bakery, the family name written above one window, a loyal terrier at their feet. Five children: Arthur dead at sixteen, in horrifying pain; Frank also lost during her lifetime. Fred Blanchard died in 1948, leaving Mary Jane a widow for almost twenty years. This is the grandmother who longed to see Betty.

Yet what can I make of her without more words and images? And what do I know of Fred Blanchard, who grew up at another windmill nearby, then managed to buy High Mill himself? That he gave his wife flowers, as another photograph of him tenderly offering her white lilies shows; that he had a famously beautiful voice, singing not only at St. Mary's in the village but at Latin Mass in the only Catholic church for miles around. Perhaps he also sang as he worked, the rhythm of the mill the background to their days: a strong whirring within, sails moving silently without.

I know that their son Frank went to Australia, for his passage is written in the manifests of vessels sailing in and out of Melbourne in the late 1920s. This was not unknown in these parts. Another postcard shows that guesthouse on the shore, only inches from the tide, a house that would inevitably be washed away. That family, dispossessed, their livelihood gone, set sail for Australia in 1919, and so did the daughter of the Hogsthorpe bicycle-maker—far away to a new life elsewhere, out of the flatlands where the bicycle was their only carriage to the vast plains on the other side of the world.

Harold and Hugh stayed in Hogsthorpe after their older siblings had gone, and after the death of their father, who tried mechanizing his mill in the 1940s, like so many other Lincolnshire millers, only to be overtaken by the advanced technology of factories. The brothers lived on, and so did Mary Jane, well into her nineties. For a long time it seemed to me that we knew more about them, from a few words in official documents or carved in gold on headstones, than we did about Hilda Blanchard.

And then one day in 1985, my mother, brother, and I decided to go back to Chapel St. Leonards to find out more. We were everywhere thwarted. The Hogsthorpe windmill was now a pottery, and the only thing we could discover about how Hilda met George—the only thing anybody would tell us—was that when Hilda Blanchard left school, she wanted to study to become a teacher. This involved catching a train from the local station at Mumby to Lincoln; and Mumby station was where George departed for various Midlands destinations. Fred Blanchard, kind Fred Blanchard, concerned about his daughter's welfare, thinks of George Elston, possibly the only regular railway passenger in these parts. Mr. Blanchard asks Mr. Elston—to whom he is presumably still delivering bread—to keep an eye on Hilda through her first journeys. And George does.

A bus connects Chapel to Hogsthorpe to Mumby, though George is a brisk, wiry sort of man who likes the roving life and sea air, striding for miles with his suitcase, so perhaps he reaches the station on foot. Or he walks from Chapel to Hogsthorpe and waits for Hilda at the bus stop close to the windmill. They travel via a magnificent stretch of Roman road that runs straight for a mile, unique among Lincolnshire's winding lanes and hairpin bends. This road was particularly beloved of my mother, and entered my childhood mythology of great world wonders, not just for its straightness but because it was not flat. It inclined very gradually from Mumby village to the station, so that she could swoop down it at speed on her bicycle. At the bottom there was even the magic of a level crossing, and the smallest of all stations, Mumby Road, the nearest departure point for faraway towns. Look south and you were on the line to London; look north and the tracks stretched towards Louth and eventually Hull. Louth was where passengers changed for Lincoln, where Hilda would study and George caught trains for parts as foreign as Birmingham, Liverpool, and Leicester.

The crossing is still there, and traces of those tracks. Stand there and you see a perfect diagram of receding perspective, the parallel lines converging at a vanishing point on the green horizon. Down to the south went my mother's friend Pat to a new life in London.

And one day she herself would take the line north towards Edinburgh, disappearing forever from this landscape.

The London and North Eastern Railway still has the intertwined initials LNER scrolling in brass script across old stations on that line. Modest trains, sometimes only a couple of coaches, would trundle through ever-smaller stations all through the county: Tumby Woodside, Thimblehall, Bag Enderby, Mareham le Fen. Mumby Road was on the Mablethorpe Loop to Louth, which ran between several little stations—Willoughby, Saltfleetby, more Viking names—some of them scarcely half a mile apart. The train moved slowly off towards Mablethorpe, where passengers often had to wait for a connection. Even the fastest journey through these twenty or so miles of level fields, where the train felt like a ship sailing upon open water, took nearly an hour. And then there was a change to Lincoln, so that George and Hilda's journey may have taken twice that time. Two hours in a closed carriage, with no side corridor; once these trains moved off, you were confined in that knee-to-knee compartment.

The station has flower beds and hanging baskets and a small office where the tickets emerge from a round dip between the glass window and the counter. Hilda and George wait on iron benches by the line, the scent of new-mown hay in the air, for it is harvest time and the beginning of the new student year. George takes an interest in Hilda's studies; Hilda is amused by his rapid wit and his driving energy, always off to the larger world somewhere else, not tethered to the spot. And he has been abroad as a soldier. There is only one train back on a Friday evening, after the week's selling of soap and attending of lectures. They take it home together.

Or is it a hedgerow romance, two people out in country lanes? They meet secretly in the fields, or walking on the sands after their first encounter on the train. Veda is at home with her elderly mother; Fred Blanchard must also be avoided. Or perhaps they run into each other by chance at the Vine. It is a mishap, a disaster, a crime. It is something, or it is nothing. There were only those two documents upon which to hang a private life: the birth certificate and the adoption agreement. They only say that life went wrong.

The birth of children "out of wedlock" was so common in Lincolnshire at that time that the local newspaper never scrupled to name names in reporting the maintenance claims at Louth Magistrates' Court. Thus Maud Branderby, unwed mother at Aby, sues Jack Price, laborer of Spilsby, for unpaid dues owing in the case of their son William, born June 1925; and so on. There was no question of confidentiality; the pleas were held in open court, attended by reporters, and referred to as bastardy cases. They sometimes involved a broken promise of marriage, or the breach of a pledge given to the woman's father, who appears as an irate witness. Occasionally the father has vanished and the case is uncontested; the mother receives justice but no money.

Hilda was by no means the only unmarried mother in her neighborhood. Children born on the wrong side of the sheets, in the period phrase, were brought up by neighbors, aunts, vicars, grandmothers, commonly believing their mothers were their older sisters. Some vanished from the public record, absorbed into the family this way and often concealed during a census. Others were not so lucky. There are applications for poor relief around this time from young women whose families have thrown them out, or who are working as servants in grand Lincolnshire houses where the master has molested them. One girl from Aby is dismissed, outrageously, by her mistress on these very grounds. Another from Mablethorpe travels all the way to London to give birth to her son in a Salvation Army home so that nobody knows. A third follows suit, but immediately gives up her child, having no friends or family to rely upon.

Secrecy was abetted by silence. Whole villages, and later council estates, would keep a family's secrets on the grounds that it was nobody's business. And in any case, familiarity bred tolerance. So many babies were born where parents could not marry, could not afford to marry, or never wished to be married in the first place, that the situation was known up and down the country.

It seems to have been no different among the English middle

classes, except that they contrived more complicated fictions. The writer Rebecca West had a decade-long affair with the married novelist H. G. Wells. Like Hilda, she was twenty-one when their son, Anthony, was born; Wells found her lodgings in a quiet seaside town. Many years later, when they parted, she officially adopted her own son, who had been led to believe he was her nephew. As late as 1947, when Anthony West was in his thirties, his mother suppressed an article in *Time* magazine identifying his actual parents.

Hilda was hardly alone in giving birth to the child of a married man, but her story has strange aspects. Given the time span of the documents, she must have been in touch with George for at least four years from first to last (if the adoption agreement is in fact a full stop). Their daughter goes back and forth between them at least once. There are no records of any appeal for maintenance, although money might have been informally given, and it seems as if Grace has been fully gathered into family life at the Blanchard mill. Having survived like this for three years, Hilda might be expected to keep on living with her daughter. Equally, George, married to Veda, might be expected to keep as far away as possible, to have nothing to do with Grace (or Hilda), and certainly not to long for his daughter. Public records suggest that it is highly unusual for a father to sue for his child in bastardy cases, and perhaps just as unusual for a married couple to adopt the child born of the husband's infidelity. It seems that both sides wanted Grace, if at different times, before she was Betty.

There they are, living the briefest of walks away from each other through long fields of barley and of rye. Chapel and Hogsthorpe are so close that modern houses, strung along the road, more or less connect them, so that the proximity now feels shattering. Surely this could only have made things more agonizing after the adoption. Every time Hilda went to the beach, she was brushing close to her child. If she went to Stow's Stores, she could have bought stamps from Betty Elston. If she visited the Vine in the summer season, she could have been served by her own daughter. Except that Hilda Blanchard was no longer there.

A year after Veda's death in 1967, when it could cause no more pain, my mother wrote again to the solicitor in Spilsby enquiring about her birth mother. He had no answers himself, but applied to Katherine Moore, niece of the Chapel dressmaker, passenger on that fateful bus, witness for Veda at the signing of the adoption agreement—Miss Moore, who was still alive.

"I telephoned Miss Moore," he reported to my mother, "as, although she is long retired, she still lives locally and she did live for many years in Chapel. She remembered the case clearly and told me that Mr. Elston was both your adoptive father and your natural father. She also said that your mother, Hilda Blanchard, came from

Hogsthorpe and that her family were millers and bakers. Miss Moore did not know whether there were any family still living in Hogsthorpe. But she recalled that Hilda Blanchard left Lincolnshire soon after the adoption was agreed. She does not remember where."

12

Family Portrait

What is wrong with this picture? Or perhaps the question should be: What is wrong with these people, a family of four making an appearance in an elegant apartment and yet at such strange odds as to undermine all semblance of unity? The scene is set for a conventional nineteenth-century portrait: mother, father, and two daughters in spotless pinafores, comfortable, well nourished, at leisure in their blue-and-gold salon, the clock serenely ticking, daylight polishing the gilded frame of the mirror. But the painting is as complex and divided as the group it portrays. The female figures on the left occupy most of the space (and perhaps the rest of the apartment) while the father on the right has withdrawn, or been sent, to his corner of the room. He turns his back, a brown

study of detachment, barricaded in an armchair, a man on the edge of the family as well as the painting.

The wife is a model of rectitude, rising above whatever injurious conditions her husband has imposed. Her hand, braced on the table, is as tense as her face. Somehow she has managed to keep up appearances in spite of his behavior, or so the evidence implies: the smart furnishings, the girls' brushed hair and immaculate frocks, her own trim black dress, in comparison to his slack jacket—all are her accomplishments. She keeps firm hold of the fair-haired child, a picture of innocence who seems to be aware of nothing except the instruction to be polite and stand straight. Her sister's hands are tensed at her waist, as if she were ready to leap from the chair and be off (like the dog). The father's hand forms a fist.

Degas's masterpiece is very nearly the size of life, and fully as profound. It hangs in the Musée d'Orsay in Paris, a riddling confrontation that continues to polarize its audience, putting each of us on the spot. One child stares directly at us, tacit acknowledgment that this is the kind of formal portrait we are used to, where the subject looks back from an image made and meant for public viewing. But everyone else turns away. The adults are deliberately ignoring each other, as well as their own offspring. The mother looks resolutely into the distance; the father gives her—and us— the cold shoulder. In no other period portrait does a sitter turn his back on the viewer in this way. To pose for a portrait is to appear in public, which this man sullenly refuses. The child in the middle may be torn between them, inviting the question: Whose side are you on?

The black-clad matriarch is Degas's aunt Laura, the girls his cousins Giulia and Giovanna, and the man his Italian uncle, Count Gennaro Bellelli. The scene takes place in their Florentine apartment around 1858. Although Laura is actually pregnant in this portrait, she and her husband lived in perpetual schism, not helped by the recent death of her father, whose portrait, also by Degas, hangs on the wall beside her head. The Bellellis' terrible relationship was well known to other family members. Some loathed Gennaro as dishonorable and lazy; others thought Laura, forever dissatisfied, was partly to blame. She was quite open about the misery of their marriage, confiding to her nephew that the Count's "horrible nature" would one day be the death of her.

This is what Degas sees and depicts. He did not paint this family portrait, as he called it, in the usual way. Many separate drawings were made of each person: Laura and her daughters on their own, then together; the Count in his velvet chair. The final composition was probably painted in Paris over several years for the annual Salon. Although it received no attention from the press, it is by general consent the crowning achievement of Degas's youth, all its individual narratives drawn together in a psychological masterpiece: a novel in paint.

Paintings, unlike books, don't divide between fiction and nonfiction. But this one tells a story that invites interpretation. Perhaps Laura is justly aggrieved, a dignified woman stoically enduring a terrible marriage, an unwanted pregnancy, and the loss of her father. She is doing everything, looking after the house and the children and even having to stand, in her condition, while Bellelli slouches in idle indifference. Or perhaps the Count is understandably in retreat from her martyred accusations, from all the disappointments she holds against him, and those girls are complicit. The blameless family dog is just trying to edge out of the scene. Of all the many things that could be said about this picture of oppression and suppression, of knowledge and innocence, not the least is this unique interplay between public and private. These people are posing for a portrait, a public record of themselves, of what they looked like separately and together in the family lineup, and yet the pull is inward. Inner and outer are dislocated, two different things; a performance of unity betrayed by aversion.

Given that the people of two villages knew their secret, I wonder how the Elstons presented themselves to the outer world. Did they appear as a family, were they seen together in public? George avoided both Chapel and Hogsthorpe, and the scene of what some may have regarded as his crime, by leaving Lincolnshire every Monday. He could lead a double life between two worlds that never overlapped. Veda stayed at home, without the use of a telephone, ignorant of his wanderings and whereabouts. She attended church every Sunday with Betty; but George never joined them, and had nothing to do with the church committee, the servicemen's canteen, or the tea meetings she ran for charity. Veda braved the eyes of the villagers as George rarely did, alone, protected only by their compassion or pity.

In a family of three there will generally be two sitters and one photographer. So it is with the Elstons, and George is invariably in charge of the camera. In the family album, the word *Snapshots* casually embossed on its black leather cover, he brings his wife and daughter together. Here are Veda and Betty in conversation, posing in the garden, or even—in one precious shot—standing with their arms around each other. George and Betty are a far rarer proposition, only appearing together when she is little. Indeed, most of the photographs in the album show Betty alone. She rides a birthday bicycle in the back garden, sits on the notorious swing holding up the *Happy Days* annual, stands next to the little aviary. The

photographs of her stop, tellingly, around the age of thirteen, and there is just that one before the age of three, the puzzling shot of George and Grace at the beach in the back. The images begin and end at exactly the same time as the closeness between father and daughter.

There is only one photograph of George and Veda alone together as a couple. Could it be the only one ever taken? Perhaps George did not like to concede control of the camera. At any rate, Betty is behind the lens today, Veda sweetly smiling back at her daughter, the soft hair, now white, in a crown around that gentle face. George stands behind, hand on hip, staring away to the side. He does not smile at his child or put an arm around his wife. This is not an accidental pose but a deliberate response to the occasion. What is wrong with this picture, it seems, is that George is a reluctant performer; there, but averted.

I have stood where he stands, in that high-hedged garden with the scent of leaves in the air, trying to imagine myself into that scene. It is 1948. My mother is briefly home from art college and George is wearing a three-piece suit for the event. In the evening, he will leave the two of them behind and walk across the fields for a drink, smoking hard as he goes. Nothing in the landscape has changed, barely a hedge; there is the worn path, the church bell sounding out as always over the early-autumn brambles, and yet I cannot think we are in the same country. The past diminishes into halftones. George and Veda Elston cast their actual living shadows into the future through this photograph, seventy years ago, and yet because they are not in color it is easy to see them as ghosts already, moving around in half-darkness. George in particular is always dark: dark-faced, dark-eyed, an oblique character edging out of the scene. Look closely at family albums and these revelations emerge across time, in the way people hold or withhold themselves, heading for the shadows, appearing or disappearing from the pages. There is a truth in the fact that there are no images of Betty after she leaves school, as if she had no further life. And in the fact that George only appears happy in a few rare shots with men. He never smiles in the company of Veda or Betty.

Black-and-white photographs seal people into a colorless world, as if they saw life that way too. The mind knows this is false, but the optic nerve is fooled into finding these figures less real, immediate, vital. Monochrome turns the present into the past, makes the past look even more distant. I look at Veda in that shot, and though I know that Edwardian stoicism wouldn't have stanched the agony of George's betrayal any more than it would now, the photograph puts her emotions even further beyond my reach. All that boot-blacking and mangling and cake baking—was it enough of a comfort, did it soothe the piercing wound of Grace's birth? Twenty years of marriage without a child, and then the arrival of George's baby with another woman. Hilda in Veda's head all the time, so close by that they might accidentally meet. Imagine living by the beach where Betty was kidnapped; no wonder she never went there. My mother remembers the day they all forgot Veda's birthday; it passes just as keenly to me. George, who always managed to buy her daffodils—from where?—in late January, simply produced nothing, and only at the very end of the day did Veda mention, quietly, that this had been her birthday. I can only assume she felt the sharpness of it, as did my mother, as do I now. To commemorate Veda's life, Elizabeth planted thousands of daffodil bulbs in the grounds of Chapel school for the pupils to pick on Mother's Day each year, so that no future mother would ever be forgotten.

How did Veda carry herself, how did she feel inside, in the long years since that early photograph with George and her sister in the Yorkshire countryside? There were upheavals: from one county to another, from one home to another. But her husband was never out of work, and they somehow got by. I don't suppose there was ever a sudden terrible outburst of shattering news. Perhaps Veda even suspected her husband's infidelity. She managed to carry off the harvest festivals and charity whist drives, the parish meetings and years of running the soldiers' canteen, ever practical, constant, enduring. But did she have any rights in George's eyes, did she have any say in which direction to take, this gentle Mrs. Which-Way? Perhaps she loved George enough to forgive him, or thought it her Christian duty, or, like so many other husbands and wives, had simply no choice.

I have her cookery book, blue-lined with a desiccated cloth binding, more than a hundred years old, containing recipes for tea meetings, which generate new recipes in turn. Granny Crawford's daisy scones; seed cake with half an ounce of peel from Mrs. Richardson (mother of Pat); coconut biscuits from Mrs. Paterson (wife of the doctor who delivered Grace). The book is a testament to frugality—no money, food, or pages ever wasted. Even the inside cover holds recipes for furniture polish made with turpentine, and camphorated chloroform for toothache. It begins in the newlywed Bradford days with more exotic fare—cup puddings served with gin sauce, Bolton pudding steamed in a basin lined with damsons—and runs all the way to instructions for plain scones given by a nurse at Edinburgh Royal Infirmary, where Veda is hemming bandages, still making herself useful half a century later. The slowness of life is echoed in her patient copperplate, the old seasonal certainties written into the calendar. Make marmalade in the first week of March. Buy pickled hams on 1 November; they will take twenty-eight days to salt. Social history passes through these pages. For rheumatism there is oil of amber, now banned; laudanum mixed with camphor for sprains. The Second World War comes and goes—a toffee recipe gives the exorbitant cost in ration stamps for condensed milk—and Christmas recurs with fractional improvements to the pudding as ingredients come back into circulation. Betty's ten-year-old handwriting momentarily appears and, out of the blue, Hilda Green's rules for crab and cucumber sandwiches. Unlike all the others, this entry remains unticked.

I search for Veda's voice in occasional turns of phrase. "To make cheesecake, boil butter and lemon until they are as honey in a jar." I find her in the condition of the book itself, pristine despite half a century in a working kitchen. The humblest of objects characterize their owners. Veda's Vicks jar was empty of everything except its scent, yet she kept it for my pleasure.

It comes to me suddenly that the couple in Betty's photograph are my grandparents, that I am of them. Yet I cannot feel it for George, whose bloodline I extend. Veda is the only person to whom I am bound. Of course, this is because I knew her, and can reconstitute the old photographs, turning her back into full color; but also because she is so far the injured party that I am taking sides. And how easy this is, since Veda shows no signs of Laura Bellelli's rigid resentment, in life or in photographs. In fairy tales, she would have treated Betty cruelly; in reality, she seems to have been entirely accepting.

Whatever she feels towards George in that picture, Veda looks out with love to her daughter. The daughter who has stitched the clothes Veda is wearing. The daughter who has become her friend and dispelled the monotony. At the very least there is another story to hear when Betty comes to live with the Elstons, another unfurling narrative and telling of daily news, of feelings and experiences beyond her own. Perhaps it was not George but Betty Veda loved enough to forgive him.

As for George, his public face is with other men—fellow travelers, factory managers, locals in the Vine. There is a photograph of him on a jaunt with two local farmers and Dr. Paterson. He was a Freemason, joining a lodge in Liverpool that was about as far from home as he could get, but gave it up when my mother was born, possibly out of conscience or because he could no longer afford the dinners. When my mother turned twenty-one and the duties laid out in the adoption agreement were over, he became a Freemason once more. He was sixty-seven by now, and retired. What he did then, other than the usual round of walking the beach, collecting the newspaper, and buying a drink, I have no idea. Barely a single sample of his handwriting survives beyond signatures and occasional phrases. He would be almost a blank if it weren't for his war records, his Freemason's certificate, and an account of his funeral in the *Skegness Times*, pointedly reporting my mother's absence. I can't even discover who he worked for, though his lodge was near Lever Brothers in Port Sunlight. Veda and George leave no correspondence, whereas I have literally thousands of letters from my mother, beginning the moment I left home for university and continuing ever since. She has not lived the day until it is recorded; she has not loved without putting it in words. She is in my story, and I in hers, so deeply that I can scarcely believe she came from a household of such detachment and silence.

George is opaque. He lost Hilda Blanchard, if he ever had her; but who knows whether he felt anguish, fury, indifference, relief. Maybe he longed to know what became of her, felt increasing bitterness, or was simply grateful that he and his wife were spared the horror of running into her in public, on the beach, in a lane, at Stow's Stores. George and Veda recover themselves. All continues. And they must keep up appearances, for everyone around them knows.

Granny Crawford had to know, for into her old age arrived a small child of three. The Greens knew; as did their daughter, Rebe, although she never breathed a word. Lizzie Cornell, keeper of an entire village's secrets, obviously knew, and so did Dr. Paterson, having brought Grace into the world. Bert Parrish, cycling around, cigarette in mouth, presumably communicated the knowledge to his daughters, which is why the two girls were suddenly barred from the door. Mr. and Mrs. Stow knew, and the Simpsons, and the Robinsons. But they all kept silent.

And this continued when we returned to Chapel in 1985 in the hope of discovering something more about Veda, George, and Hilda, and how my mother could have been passed between them. Every door was opened to us and then politely closed. We sat over tea, walked in people's gardens, paid our respects to everyone still living and known to my mother, including some of these very neighbors, but nobody told us a thing.

Through photographs, we have relationships with people unknown. A shot of my family might mean something to you just as well as to me. It is almost a test of human solidarity. Every portrait comes before our eyes like life, and when the scene involves the ties of love or blood, we can hardly help applying our own experience. Even the universal school photograph is a set of relationships, between photographer, pupils, and circumstance. The picture of George and Veda in the garden is mine, and intimate, but public too, as open to your response as to mine. I have shown it to others without identifying the couple; some think George is semidetached but protective, as if shielding his wife from a draft. Most think that he is reluctant or evasive.

In her classic work *On Photography*, Susan Sontag insists that photography alienates us from direct experience, that it denies continuity, atomizes reality. She believes photographs are merely an illusion of knowledge, that they cannot offer the truths that come only from narration and words. But this cannot be entirely right. Truth is apparent in the way people choose to present themselves to the lens, their recoil and shyness, their directness and élan; in the accidental image and the propaganda shot where people hold fast to staged poses; above all in the billions of self-portraits in which each photographer shows time and again how she or he wishes to be seen and known.

Truth is there in the very act of appearing before the camera. Veda, we intuit, addresses herself to Betty quite naturally in the garden, open to the family occasion. George strikes his semidetached pose, choosing to behave this way. This is the 1940s, after all, and shutter speeds are still anxiously slow; you had to lock yourself into position. The American writer Ralph Waldo Emerson called it a kind of rigor mortis, every muscle more rigid by the moment as he stood still for the camera. The result, he thought, could never be more than a mask. Certainly, photographs offer only as much as the subject is willing to give. And yet there is something true about this scene in Chapel, which is the way that George chooses to turn aside from it, or from the person who holds the camera.

They have gone out to the garden before or after lunch because the light is better for photography. Perhaps it is autumn, looking at George's suit; or perhaps it is spring, and the cold frame by Veda's feet is bringing on the season's new vegetables, cucumbers or cabbages for her table. Veda inclines towards her daughter—and her husband—apparently touched to be photographed. George complies, but only on sufferance, almost sidestepping the idea of a family portrait. Here he stands with Veda, before Betty. He does not look his daughter in the eye. This will be the last photograph. We look back at the past and discover the shape of the future.

My mother says it is all as far away to her now as the toy theater of her childhood, miniature and remote. Except for the country bus, which remains large in memory. But here in this little picture is the proof of how enduring their life's crisis really was in the click of a shutter. That afternoon with her parents, back home, Betty is trying and failing to bring the family tight together again, to round it out in a portrait so small you could hold it in the palm of your hand.

13

Birthday Presents

This is the scene in another garden, fixed by a flash of shock. It is the morning of my mother's sixtieth birthday. We are sitting outside the cottage in the Scottish Borders to which my parents have now moved, and although it is August, wind is already troubling the Albertine roses she manages to coax out of the chill black soil. We are having peaches for breakfast, still rare to us in the North, and on the table is a great gathering of envelopes, the handwriting of her many friends all over the country familiar to us from years of close correspondence. But among them is one in an unknown hand, with odd loops and dots and an unusual slant, perhaps foreign. Inside it is a letter that rewrites her story once more.

It came from somebody signing herself Susan and was couched

in almost breezily familiar terms, announcing that she and her sister were now in London, but due to come to Edinburgh, where they very much hoped to meet her. She did not identify the two of them and gave not a hint of the relationship she clearly felt they had with my mother. We pored over the page for clues—in the color of the ink, the size of the sheet, the character of the handwriting. Was the writer young or old? Were these women from overseas? Probably remote second cousins, I insisted, longing to protect my mother from disappointment. We felt exhilaration edged with fear.

For of course it had always seemed possible that there were relatives somewhere, perhaps even close relatives, someone left to tell the story. And the fact that these people announced themselves as now being in London implied arrival from somewhere far away.

My mother endured a month of nearly intolerable suspense, constantly thinking of the impending meeting, trying to hold fast to the idea that these two women would turn out to be distant relatives at best. Their surnames were Baker and Beale. Whoever they were, they presumably knew more about the family history—and perhaps her origins—than she did. Members of our Scottish family who had hitherto known nothing at all about my mother's early life and adoption, including her sisters-in-law, rather astonishingly, were told that some news was imminent. We were all drawn into the puzzle of the letter—the return address was a Bloomsbury hotel where the staff could offer us no information about the two guests, who had already checked out by the time we rang—and into a cycle of endless speculation.

At last the day came. The arrangements had been made by letter, an impossibly antique situation as it seems now. The three women were to converge at a hotel near Edinburgh Zoo, which already had a resonance for our family, as it was where Rebe Green had once taken us for that elaborate high tea. My mother drove from the Borders into the city. She was early. While she waited, an oceanic turbulence began to rise within her: she could not come face-to-face with these people, whoever they were, because the dam might break and everything held back for decades would overwhelm her.

Just as she was growing breathless and choked, with thoughts of running away, two women walked into the foyer. Both recognized her immediately. "You look just like Hilda." The surrounding world fell silent, as it seemed for an age, before the younger woman spoke again, to clarify: "You look just like our mother."

Susan had an Australian accent; she was Hilda's third daughter. The effect was as devastating, in another way, as the childhood encounter on the bus. If we hadn't allowed ourselves to imagine that these correspondents could be as close as cousins, we had certainly suppressed all hope that they might be half sisters, able to bring tidings of their mutual mother. But one wave arriving on the tide met another departing. Just as my mother met her sisters for the first time, so she discovered that Hilda Blanchard was dead.

She wrote to me:

A new family calendar is to be entered up, one which records this: yesterday, 11th September, is the anniversary of the death of my mother Hilda, in 1974, aged 69. Her birthday: 27 November 1904.

Her three daughters' birthdays:
Grace: 8 August 1926, when she was 21
Judith: 16 December 1933, when she was 29
Susan: 14 June 1942, when she was 37

This is only known to me since 3 days ago, September 1986, when I went to meet two unknown sisters, their existence undreamt of all these years.

These were the rudimentary facts. Soon after the adoption, Hilda left Hogsthorpe on an assisted passage to Australia. On a sheep station in the outback, she met and married a man named Lance Lakey. They had two daughters and four grandchildren, and she had eventually become an English teacher in a secondary school in

Melbourne many years after she took her first journey to study teaching in Louth. Hilda Blanchard had sailed away from that fraction of Lincolnshire out across the world, making the vast transition from one continent to another during which a person may seem to change form or be lost altogether, starting a new life, shucking off the old one.

The existence of my mother was equally unknown to Judith and Susan, at least until the early 1970s. Hilda did not tell them that she had another child until late in her life. History says she may have been unusual in telling them at all; so many infants have been omitted from their mothers' narratives. But, of course, Grace was not an infant: she had lived with Hilda for three years. And although Hilda never spoke of her, she saw Grace's face every day. On the table by her bed stood a black-and-white photograph of a fair-haired girl smiling among tulips in a garden. For some reason Judy never asked about her, but Susan did. She was apparently a child from long ago.

My tactful mother did not like to barrage her new sisters with questions in those first days, since memories of Hilda understandably upset them; and they were more interested in the present, in what my mother was like, how she had lived, who we were. But I was in my early twenties and avid for knowledge. I wanted to know how my mother had come into the world, what Hilda felt about this first daughter, why nobody had tried to find her all these years. Even though they were about to set sail for Australia again, my new aunts said very little, being tactful too. Everyone was so polite that George wasn't even mentioned.

But we did learn that Hilda had sailed back to England three times, in 1933 when my mother was seven, in 1938 when Judy was four, and in 1947 when Susan was five. She returned to the mill with Lance for nine months the first time, and then without him for almost a year in 1938. Hilda was once again so close to her lost daughter. Surely she must have seen her somewhere in those wide open flatlands, on the beach, in a lane, perhaps on a bus. At one point, Hilda was working at Butlin's to make money for her family; the bus to Skegness Grammar stopped there en route. The adoption agreement could hardly control fate. The possibility of sightings obsessed me, and I still take comfort from the fragile hope that Hilda and Grace, now Betty, must have been reconnected by sight, held in each other's eyes, however briefly.

For my mother to meet her half sisters in 1986 was also a matter of agonizing chance.

It was twenty years since she had made that first and last attempt to discover her origins, returning to Lincolnshire to find her birth certificate in Spilsby. This, of course, gave her mother's name, and the solicitor had offered a vague intimation that there were

Blanchards still living in those parts. But my mother went no further than her courage took her; friends suggested that it would be idealistic to imagine that she would be welcomed into Hilda's life at this stage, and in any case she had long since left the area. Loyalty to Veda precluded more protracted enquiries, and it seemed on both sides a closed account. The finality of the adoption agreement signed in 1929 certainly seemed to seal the Blanchards' lips.

But in the autumn of 1985, my mother and brother had gone on another discreet foray to Lincolnshire to see what they could discover. In Hogsthorpe, the windmill had shrunk to a stump, the mill house was harled, the bakery now a display room for the pottery. They lingered here a long time, noticing the structure of the old walls, wondering how it must have been and, in her case, straining for any lost memory. These were the doorways she must have walked through, but there was no sense of past atmosphere.

My brother drew out the potter in casual ways to reveal the only thing he knew about the long-ago owners, which was that a grandson still lived over the road at a nearby farm. But they passed on through Hogsthorpe, my mother resisting my brother's eagerness to call directly on this man. She felt it a total impossibility to arrive out of the blue, the family skeleton. What if he did not know the story? The ensuing shock and burden of explanation and embarrassment would have been an ordeal all round.

She bought a pot and planted it, later, with an evergreen.

I joined them at Chapel, where we went round the village visiting all those surviving acquaintances. Even when we mentioned Hilda, and asked for any kind of explanation of her relationship with George, or George's with Veda, they all remained resolutely silent. Among them were Eve Paul, daughter of the old coastguard, now in her nineties, and the Elstons' former neighbor Mrs. Simpson, also in her nineties. Eve would only say that George was a very difficult man and that Veda was a saint. Jessie Simpson at least allowed herself to remember that Betty was a tug-of-war child, back and forth, and that there was a terrible hullabaloo in Chapel St. Leonards when she was suddenly stolen from the Elstons. This was the first time we ever heard of the kidnap. But she would add nothing more and visibly recoiled from the word *adoption*.

But Mrs. Simpson did tell her daughter about the visit, and it was this woman, almost a stranger to this tale, and to whom we will always be indebted, who took the plunge and told a friend in the Blanchard family. Which is how the news of my mother's existence, and of her visit to Hogsthorpe, came to reach her half sisters on the other side of the world. One person thought that sixty years of silence was enough, that this unspoken civility, or shame, or mutual tact, or whatever it was, maintained by centrifugal force across the globe, must now cease. The statute of limitations had run out.

It was too late, of course. Too late for Hilda Blanchard; too late for Fred and for Mary Jane, who had died in 1969 at the age of ninety. And it was too late for my mother in respect of them all. She would never meet any of them now—an agony compounded by the sudden realization that she so easily might have. She would never know what Hilda was like, what she felt and said and knew, the cast of her thought, the tone of her voice. But at least there was a face, arriving in the form of a photograph.

Hilda's identity had been an enigma all these years, curiosity on my mother's part having gradually lessened with time, and especially in the great life-change of having her own children. But now here she was, in a picture sent from Australia by our loving new aunts. Hilda is coming home, arriving at Port Melbourne in February 1948. She is forty-four, smiling beautifully, in one of those boxy wartime jackets, artificial silk and heavy tailoring against the ocean weather en route. I look at her and see my mother.

The advent of Judy and Susan brought other new relatives too, good kind people dotted around Lincolnshire, all warmly welcoming to my mother. Among them was the oldest surviving member of the family. Her name was Fanny Willson, known as Great-Aunt Fanny. She was the sister of Grandma Blanchard.

Fanny was a hundred and one years old, a woman of extraordinary clarity and fortitude. My mother went to visit her, taking a friend to act as scribe, for this first encounter was too momentous to be undermined by the practicalities of a tape recorder. But it was not the first time that they had met. "My Betty!" was Fanny's astonishing greeting to the long-lost child she had last seen more than half a century before—in her own home. For it was to Fanny's house that Betty was taken during the kidnap.

Fanny was astonished herself, and not just at the sudden reappearance of a beloved child she'd never imagined seeing again. There was another reason. Like Judy, like Susan, she did not know that Betty had lived all the time in complete ignorance of the Blanchards, or that her early life had vanished, entirely erased. Her amazement formed itself in Lincolnshire dialect: "After you not having a birth certificate! After you never knowing any of it! After everything being total mystery and a blank, the first years all unaccounted. Never a photograph when other children had! No talk of when you were little. No mother ever secretly telling about your birth pangs, though yours had plenty of a different kind. Well, you know now that you have a family, otherwise you'd think you had no one."

She began with the annals of that family. The names of her thirteen siblings were recited in careful order, Fanny laughing at her self-imposed memory test. She spoke of her years in service at a stately home through the First World War, of walking to the village church on her wedding day and coming home to an afternoon off, before returning to silver-service duties. Fanny needed almost no encouragement to unloose many family memories, speaking in plain, unemotional sentences that seemed to testify all the more to the starkness of our common mortality. With the long look-back of a century's living, the more poignant losses were naturally uppermost in her mind. The sudden death of her husband; the terrible discovery of her only son, Billy, by then in his fifties, drowned by accident in a hospital bath. She spoke with much sympathy of the many griefs of Grandma Blanchard and the minute-by-minute last hours of Grandpa Blanchard, as well as the days preceding their son Arthur's death. We can hardly realize the way illness crept up in a time when the doctor's visit was a luxury only to be indulged in as a last resort, often too late.

Eventually Fanny came to my mother, remembering her as a fair-haired infant in the bakery, loved by all. A little child whose father wanted her, shuttled between the houses of her mother and father until she was smuggled into Fanny's own. This had happened in the autumn of 1929. Betty—she was apparently Betty by now—had been "claimed back" from George, taken off the sands at Chapel. She was brought to Fanny's house near the town of Alford, where they bought her "new clothes all through." Red clothes, too, not the blue she wore with the Elstons. And who knows how long they might have managed to live there together, with nobody in Alford recognizing the child. "But then the police came knocking, and you was gone."

Fanny, on this first visit, remembered Hilda Blanchard as very intelligent and with nearly auburn hair (a point on which the monochrome photographs were of course mute), just like my mother as an adult. As well as family affairs, she talked about her working life, still referring to her employers as "the masters and mistresses." My mother wrote a letter about the encounter.

Those days of English pastoral life, beginning in the reign of Queen Victoria, were hard by our standards, but Fanny, like so many very aged people, says that work is the secret of long life. She repeatedly said that she couldn't believe in her own longevity, or that she would live to see Hilda's lost daughter. I was equally incredulous, and suspended in a realm of feeling that you can perhaps imagine—a compound of past and present brought together in this amazing personage connecting the centuries.

My mother drew up a startling timeline of Great-Aunt Fanny.

Born in 1886.

Queen Victoria still reigning, Prime Minister Lord Salisbury, Grover Cleveland President of the USA, 4 years before was the fall of Bismarck.

1—When Fanny was one, Edinburgh had its first street lighting

3—Eiffel Tower built

6—Tennyson died. Hardy wrote *Tess of the d'Urbervilles.*

7—Tchaikovsky wrote Symphonie "Pathétique."

12—Marie Curie discovered radium and Zeppelin invented airships.

13—Boer War begun, in which George Elston fought.

15—Victoria died.

17—Wright brothers flew for the first time.

24—Tolstoy died.

28—Great War began.

40—Grace Blanchard born.

43—Fanny sheltered me after the kidnap.

Soon after this first visit, my mother arranged for my brother and me to meet Fanny. She was so fragile and fine, the skin practically translucent over her bones, light fingers gesturing expressively as she spoke. We made a tape recording of every word, in its concise simplicity. None of us mentioned the relationship between Hilda and George, about whom Fanny knew nothing. But we did ask about our mother's arrival in the world; she replied with devastating directness.

"I did not know Hilda was expecting a baby. I was visiting my mother in Alford and she said to me, have you been to Hogsthorpe lately? I said no, she says I wish you would go, I says, why, Mother, I have nothing to go for? She was worried so she got my older sister Lizzie to go, and she went to Hogsthorpe for the weekend and stayed there with Grandma Blanchard. At the time she was there, your grandma kept a shop, and Lizzie bought some things from out the shop. Well, that night Hilda went to a dance and then she came home and went up to bed. Next morning she got up and took her mother and father a cup of tea, Lizzie told me, and then she went back to bed. In the afternoon your grandma went upstairs to fetch some wrapping for these goods my sister had bought and as she passed her door Hilda called out, Mother, I want you, come. . . . So Grandma Blanchard went in and Hilda says, I'm having a baby. Now them's the words Grandma Blanchard told me. No, Hilda, she says, you're not! I am, I am having a baby, she says. And she opened the bedroom window and her brothers were down in the yard and she called out, will you fetch your father to me here at once? And they fetched Fred and when he sees the condition she was in, he ran and fetched the doctor and when the doctor got there, Hilda was in a state of agony. Kill it, she says to him when it was going to be born. Kill it! No, Hilda, he says, the baby will live and you will rear it here. Now I am telling you what it was, just as the words that Lizzie told me. And my sister she came back home and she says, Fanny, I was so upset and poor Mary she was so upset, and she didn't know where to put herself . . . but she says, I am thankful to say that the baby lived. And there she is now," said Fanny, gazing at my mother. "She is one of the best. I never thought I should live to tell the story, and that was the story it was."

Fanny told my weeping mother, to soften the shock, that her mother had certainly loved her. She spoke of Hilda as a lovely girl, so clever, educated at the grammar, training to be a teacher of English. But she spoke little more of her, presumably because Hilda was soon gone to Australia; and because her mind turned to Mary Jane, her sister, whose heart she understood better.

"I went about a month afterwards, to visit the mill, and there you were in the carriage, cooing, beautiful. I can remember the old bakehouse when you was asleep, I would come and peep at you. And when you woke up I used to go and push the pram, because they was all busy baking bread and cakes. Your grandma had a lovely new pram for you. Everything was up-to-date. She was very thorough. I can see you now in that carriage and you used to gurgle and I would wheel you about. You were a merry child and always so eager to help when you grew. They used to lift you up to fill the tarts. That wasn't long though, and then you was gone. Disappeared. I knew you up to that. It broke your grandmother's heart."

We asked about the kidnap. It seems that George and Hilda both wanted Grace. They would take her on picnics and outings together, sometimes to Chapel beach, and she passed time with them both. The to-and-fro was supposed to cease in 1929 when she finally went to the Elstons—except that she was suddenly kidnapped back. Betty was brought to Fanny's house, where it was thought that nobody would look for her, and given this disguise of new clothes. It didn't last long. "In the end you had to go with your father. The lawyer made it so your grandma was not allowed to speak to you, nor your mother, none of the family, nobody was, or to let you know you belonged to them. That was in the solicitor's agreement. And she kept her word, did your grandma Blanchard. Nor even my son Billy said a word, none of them—they all did as they were told. They all knew you, though. They used to see you at all sorts of events, but they never made themselves known. I can remember you running about, about this height, on the sands. I couldn't speak to you. And when you got older, I used to meet you at Mrs. Richardson's house when I went to visit there. You would be bicycling in from school at Skegness. Billy used to come home and say, do you know, I had a dance at Chapel tonight with Hilda's little daughter."

Mrs. Richardson: mother of Pat, Betty's school friend. Presumably this was how the Richardsons knew. But everyone kept the contract to say nothing to the child—even Harold Blanchard, with the bread basket on his arm, calling upon the neighbors. Never once did he betray himself, or any of them, with a single word that he might so easily have tossed over the hedge.

"I am so sorry I never saw my grandmother again," says my mother, on the tape, "because she took a lot of care of me."

"Well," says Fanny, "you would have been very happy if you had been brought up at the mill, because everyone was very content there together. These uncles of yours, they used to come rabbiting with Billy. My daughter had a piano, and they all were musical— the violin, the concertina, they always used to be playing and singing and enjoying themselves. And I had them every Christmas Day, your grandma was always so tired out after the Christmas baking and she was pleased they all would come. We used to take up the carpets and dance."

It pierces me to think what was taken from my mother. All the possibilities of a large and bustling family. She was a merry child then; but she became an anxious woman. The celebratory in her, strong as it is, lives inside a forest of fears.

Fanny identified the woman on the bus. She was Aunt Emma, one of Fanny's many sisters. Her intentions were benign. Compassion for Mary Jane led her to break George's despotic rules, although of course she achieved nothing by it, for, like the North Wind in Aesop's fable, she terrified Betty instead of appealing to her with the warmth of the sun.

"I suppose you wonder why I hadn't tried to discover you," my mother later wrote with characteristic self-reproach to her new sisters, never wondering why they had not tried to contact her, since they had known of her existence and even her exact location since the early 1970s. "There seems to have been a reciprocal block, operating on both sides. . . . I just looked on the past as a closed chapter, and felt that I was some other person than the one who had been Grace for those three years in another life. The Buddhists I think it is who ask their adherents to take a completely new name, really understanding the power of the word. A new orientation takes place."

My mother and her sisters are united by love, and blood, but have no shared background. They are from different continents, have disparate natures. For a while afterwards, she hesitantly questioned and they were serenely unexpansive about the past, even their own reaction to the revelation that Hilda had another daughter. They have made the long journey from Australia twice since then, and embraced my mother completely within their lives. The lost time is emblematically diminished in the gold band she wears on her middle finger: Mary Jane's wedding ring, the gift of Judy and Susan. But all I have ever really learned of Hilda herself has come much more recently from my aunts: "Her eyes were very blue, deep-set. Height 5'4". She had no accent, English, but hard to say where from—just like Betty. I never heard her shout or raise her voice. She had a soft beautiful voice. Character, strong, well educated. I would say brave as she came to a strange country." Which could as easily be a description of my mother.

Hilda set out for Australia from the Port of London on 1 February 1930, ten weeks after signing the adoption agreement. Any hopes she had of being employed as a teacher by the Australian government were flattened on arrival. They were not in need of teachers so much as domestic help for large country properties, and Hilda was sent out to the magnificent wilds of the Western District, as it was then known, to a sheep station called Mount Hesse. Here she cooked and cleaned for the Scottish Kinninmonth family, who had several children she may have taught before they were sent off to boarding school in Geelong. Among the red rocks and the parched acres of merino sheep, she met Lance, who ran the shearing machinery. They married; Judy and Susan were born.

What a translation for Hilda from Lincolnshire to the Australian landscape: unimaginably vast, ancient, sunburned, and free, with its unbounded space and crackling outback. From the low, dark drains to the immense heat and light; from Hogsthorpe to the teeming port of Melbourne, where she later lived with Lance, shiny new cars churning the ocher dust of Bourke Street, elegant buildings going up from the center out to the fledgling suburbs. But soon the work begins to dry up; Australia succumbs to the global Depression. Assisted passages virtually cease after 1930, and many of those who have only recently arrived start to depart. Hilda returns, back to the village from out of the wide-open world, but Lance could not or would not settle in Hogsthorpe. On the second visit, in 1938, Mary Jane and Fred hope that Hilda will stay, even buying her a house in Chapel, of all places, and so close to the Elstons that one imagines them forever running into each other. What were they thinking? But back to Australia she goes again. Susan sent my mother some of Hilda's old letters. In these, she writes home in a tense, practical voice. It is not hard to discern the suffering suppressed.

For several years, before she finally found a teaching position, Hilda worked in a post office.

An Australian friend once told me that his compatriots can appear incurious about the past, putting it behind them because they are always "just starting." Perhaps this is why Susan and Judy did not press their mother about the photograph by the bed. It had always been there. Susan wrote to me: "I knew it was not me or Judy, or anyone else I had ever seen a photo of, but things were just accepted. It was part of the room. I had asked who it was when I was eleven or twelve and I can still remember her soft voice with the reply, and maybe instinctively knew that that was enough." Judy, taken as a small child to stand outside 1 St. Leonard's Villas, received the same answer from her mother. Who lived there? "A little girl I once knew."

14

Out to Sea

The beach is immense. It stretches for miles in the summer haze, unchanging, perpetually modern. What I see today is exactly what Tennyson saw, and generations of my family from Granny Crawford to Veda then Betty, day by day through her childhood: the pale bronze sand beneath a soaring cobalt sky—the houseless shore in living color.

I must stop seeing their world in black and white, the way old cameras preserve it, and my mind's eye still frames it: George a dark specter, Veda a shadow in the kitchen. Imagination arranges the figures like a practiced photographer, composing scenes so they make sense, justifying each sequence with explanatory subplots. George has his way; Hilda surrenders the child and is banished;

Veda is no longer lonely. That version is as graphic and reductive as a monochrome photograph. But it was for a long time my only picture of events, constructed from clues and reinforced by emotion and instinct, until searching made a mockery of each certainty. Life reproves the imagination: look closer.

Sitting on the dune walkway, I see occasional flashes of sky in the sea and recall the ships stalled in the shallows, the airmen dropping from German planes, grapefruit spilling yellow across the beach. I picture my mother in her bright-blue dress stolen from those sands.

We came here when I was a child, long before anyone knew of the kidnap. In those days it was a simple narrative of buckets, spades, and candy floss, warm translucent waves, the peg-legged gait of a donkey ride along the shore. I remember staying at the Vine; its liquid porridge heavily doused with sugar, which was not our Scottish way, the diamond-pane windows, and the Jolly Fisherman printed on display plates in the foyer. I remember driving all the way from Edinburgh in a car without seat belts, hot red leather sucking at the backs of my knees. But I have no recollection of paddling in the fairy dell at Skegness; photographs say that we did, but they don't generate a spark. The memory has gone out. I was three, like my mother in the bakery, and she had not even the prompt of photographs or family anecdotes. It doesn't surprise me that she has nothing left except the jam.

Her life in Chapel was my childhood fable. Naturally I began to question it as an adult. Stories get better with the telling. Going through the usual travails after university, trying to find work, trapped in a first job where the vicious employer menaced his young staff, where I saw colleagues bullied and sacked on the spot, I occasionally wondered just how terrible the post office could have been under the kindly eye of Mr. Stow. I go there now, into what used to be the Stores, now an omni-purpose emporium stocked mainly out of China, and instantly realize for the very first time—what a failure of my imagination—just what a prison this is. For here is the back room where my mother sat, windowless and oppressively dark despite modern strip lighting: a freezing cave even on this summer's day. How could George have done it? How could he have wrenched her out of school, locked her away in the prime of her youth, deprived her of everything that my parents gave me—education and hope, friendship, freedom, and love?

The Vine is long past its best, getting by with alternate nights of karaoke and curry. You have to search hard to discover the old village in the tide of new holiday homes and caravan parks (one called Happy Days), but still it is just about there. The circular village green remains, and the handful of shops and cafés where the buses from Skegness still wheel round, a faint haze of sand shifting down from the strand. Walk up and over the Pulley and there is the beach, a sequence of receding strips: esplanade, shore, sea, and far horizon. The edge of the world.

Today, in high June, in the baking heat, there is not a soul here. A pub built from an old boat opens its doors on the beach; gentle winds shiver the sea grass; the water reflects the swelling cumulus above. And there is the uninterrupted stretch of sand. How could Hilda have snatched her away so easily, when there is nowhere to hide?

It seems to me that the only exit is the Pulley in the center of the village, but then I begin to walk and discover narrow clefts through which today's sun seekers pass on holiday mornings. Grace could have been whisked through any of them, straight into the waiting baker's van. For there cannot have been anything spontaneous about it, as I had always imagined. Hilda could hardly have walked my tiny mother all the way home to Hogsthorpe, still less the twelve miles to Fanny's house. There must have been a getaway vehicle, other Blanchards involved, perhaps even Mr. and Mrs. Blanchard themselves helping to save Grace from a terrible mistake. Fanny's phrase keeps coming back to me: "It broke your grandmother's heart." But why Mary Jane and not Hilda?

It was Fanny who gave the details. And they are not on the tape that we made that day, but in the written transcript of my mother's first visit to her great-aunt without us. One of those documents tossed in the tide of history, that have lain in lofts and boxes and plastic bags, that have been transported from Scotland to England, and from house to house over thirty years, now unearthed from a silt of old papers.

There must have been too many picnics, too many outings. For it seems that George promised Grandma Blanchard that he would cease all connection with Hilda if only their child could go and live with him in Chapel. "But he did not keep his promise," said Fanny. "And your grandma, she wanted you as well. It was she who claimed you off the sands. She asked two lads who were playing near you to bring you over. Then she took you away, and gave you all new clothes and brought you to my house to stay. But in the end you had to go with your father. The lawyer made it so that Grandma couldn't see you anymore. But she says, Fanny, I shall not interfere. It is Hilda's wish and I know I have all the lads at home, and she doesn't want her bringing up with the boys. And so your grandma couldn't have you."

Ever since we first learned of the kidnap in 1985, we all assumed that it was the mother and not the grandmother who had come for Betty. More bewildering is that Hilda seems not to have known anything about it, until the police came knocking at the bakery door in Hogsthorpe and Mary Jane had to own up. "Your own mother, well, then she found out where you were and came and got you again and took you away to your father and new mother, and they had you ever after. It broke your grandmother's heart."

Grandma Blanchard wanted her back and came to the beach with a plan. One of my Australian aunts now confirms it, in a different version: "Hilda had given Betty to George, gone home to Grandma alone and I guess the realisation of what had taken place must have set in very quickly. Grandma must have concluded that she could reverse this, and so, with the help of the younger boys, they decided they would go to the beach and get her back within only a few days of her going to live with George. Veda was alone with Betty on the beach, and the boys a little further along called her and she came running up. Off they all went, quickly back to the mill."

But of course it can't quite be like that. They cannot know exactly when Veda will be there; it isn't a perfect plot. The story tilts between luck and design. The younger boys were Hugh and Harold, then aged twelve and fifteen. Arthur would have been nineteen. Fanny told us of his death. "I was getting ready for church and Arthur called. Auntie, I've come to say good-bye. I am going to London to work at Gamages. Well, he'd been there only a little while when he came home, and didn't look too well, and then he was in Alford Hospital. A man from Thoresby was in too and Arthur said to him, I'll never get better. Give my love to them, and if I don't see them again I will remember them forever. He died that night, a growth in his stomach."

It is always this way—a growth, a turn, a seizure, a decline. No details. And so it still is with my mother. Nothing explicit should be asked or revealed. I do not know if this is tact, fear, or decorum. I have an Edinburgh memory of someone visiting our house who was suffering from cancer. My uncle said not to sit on his chair, perhaps it was infectious. And when my father was dying in hospital, my mother didn't want me to kiss his poor face too much. Illness was to them nameless and alien. Arthur died of a ruptured appendix, two years before the discovery of penicillin.

But still these two stories do not match. Fanny says two local boys were involved, which sits with the idea of chance and spontaneity; my aunt says two uncles were brought along to help, which complies with the notion of a plan. Mary Jane was acting alone; or with the help of her family. Betty was taken to the mill; or to Fanny's house. Mary Jane did what she did on behalf of her daughter, trying to reverse Hilda's harrowing decision; or to rescue a beloved grandchild. Or both. The only point on which they agree is that Hilda was not involved.

I sit on the raised wall that runs ten miles in either direction, and everyone who passes says hello. A group of children on a geography field trip ask questions from their questionnaire. Do I know about the floods in 1953? Of course I do, for the houses were washed away and the tide came right up to the front steps of my mother's old home. Do I think Chapel needs more money to prevent floods? I do indeed, for they are still occurring. Do I think much has changed here? Nothing at all, except for the opposing flood of caravans and the windmills of today, descendants of the old, cartwheeling away far out at sea, a rival village on the water.

As I am sitting here, the bell of St. Leonard's Church chimes midday, sounding right out across the beach to mingle with the sea air. It is a shock—always the same shock in Chapel—just how close all the buildings are to drowning. I walk over to the church.

And there, outside, stands the white stone memorial commemorating the dead of two wars. Right at the bottom of the roll of honor is *Hugh Green—Navy*. The boy who went missing, for whom his mother set a place at table all through the Second World War, without ever knowing his fate. Dismissed from the Royal Navy, Hugh had signed up as a deckhand on a merchant navy ship that departed from the Clyde on 2 January 1943 as part of a rescue convoy. The vessel sailed up towards the Northwest Passage where Franklin disappeared, and then sank without trace in the freezing waters off Nova Scotia. It is presumed that the rigging became encrusted with ice and the ship turned turtle. "Lost with all hands" is the seafaring phrase. I found Hugh's name on the war memorial at Tower Hill in London. He was just twenty.

Hilda Green was destroyed by grief and Rebe, so much the subject of my mother's childhood envy, led a solitary life in nearby Woodhall Spa. She might have been just as resistant to our enquiries as everyone else in Chapel. But it was Rebe who told us that George had been a considerable draftsman; that he'd made all the exquisite bookcases in their house and once designed a device for rolling their car headlamps in the days before the dipping of beams was invented. She dignified George Elston. Indeed, she was the only one who did not recoil from the supposed shame of Betty's adoption. And when she died, Rebe Green left what remained of the family wealth to my startled mother. Veda's adopted daughter, George's illegitimate child, she felt she had no right to any Green bequest. But my mother had been loving of Rebe, careful of her peccadilloes and respectful of her parents' memory; blood, in the end, meant less than behavior.

There was enough money to build a studio for my parents' cottage in the Borders. It was used by my father until his death and then, for many years afterwards, by my mother. It was there that she wove her homage to Tennyson's "Lady of Shalott." Instead of the standard scene, beloved of Victorian painters, in which the damsel drifts to her death in a flower-strewn barge, my mother depicted her in the tower, working at her loom, sunlight pouring through the window—the very conditions in which she wove her own tapestry; a tribute from one weaver to another.

Number 1 St. Leonard's Villas is now cracked and pebble-dashed, although the great tree is still there. I walk along the drains, over Tyler's Bridge, and on towards the village of Hogsthorpe, scenting the lime trees, watching skylarks dip down over the summer fields. Poplars stand along the horizon like tall dark stitches, tacking the land to the sky. The pulse jumps with the sudden sight of a spire, and in this extreme flatness even the wheat sheaves seem high.

The windmill is completely gone now, leaving only a ring of foundation stones. But in Hogsthorpe church, damp and medieval, remains the old parish register. Here is my mother's surprising baptismal entry, Grace Ellston Blanchard, in which Hilda, or the vicar, acknowledges George. And further back in time are the records of Hilda's own baptism, the christenings of her brothers, and their deaths, along with those of Fred and Mary Jane. The completing circle.

But there are other familiar names: the Crawford sisters, Daisy and Hilda, from the photograph of that country walk near Bradford. There is even a mention of Granny Crawford, who came to live with the Elstons. They all started life at Hogsthorpe—and so did Veda. Reading the spidery dates, I realize that Veda Elston and Mary Jane Blanchard were the same age.

When my mother first went to Lincolnshire to search for her past in 1966, she was sorry to find that the Spilsby solicitor had no further documents relating to the adoption agreement. "So it cannot be scrutinised who instigated the arrangement," wrote my mother, "which means we are in the dark as to the circumstances at that time." I am struck by her probity. She could not be sure who had gone to the solicitor's, and so she remained open-minded. Everyone else believed it was George.

We have not spoken about the agreement for decades. Talking about it is too hard for my mother. To discover who Hilda was, to see her face in photographs, to come to know Judy and Susan, that has long since been enough to cauterize her curiosity about the document, with its cruel phrases and terms, its bargaining over—bargaining with—a living child.

But I still want to know more, to see and understand it all clearly. Among the photographs sent by my Australian aunts are several showing my mother as a very small child, among fruit trees and raspberry canes, picking gooseberries, standing among cabbages, by the bakery, and so on. On the back of each picture, her name is written. Sometimes she is called Grace, sometimes Betty. Here she is living in her mother's house, and yet with her father's name. How does she suddenly become Betty? Where and when and to whom does she belong?

According to Fanny, Hilda did not know where Betty was after the kidnap, didn't even know she had been taken from the sands at first. The child was no longer living with her, after all, and she seems to have been away for work. It is the new mother who is in charge of Betty that day, Veda who raises the fearful alarm; who calls George back from the Midlands to search for her, and to summon the police, who come knocking in Hogsthorpe. And then Grandma Blanchard is forced to confess that she has taken Betty, who is safe and sound with Fanny. Hilda now has the horror of retrieving her daughter and taking her back to the Elstons all over again, holding her, saying good-bye forever—once more.

Again it is Fanny who tells what happens next, in that written transcription.

"Your grandma brought you to me. Then when Hilda got to know, she went to the lawyer and had this document all made out, and sent it to Grandma Blanchard. George wanted you, and your grandma, she wanted you as well. So Hilda goes to the solicitor to settle it all, and Grandma never interfered again." Perhaps there never would have been such a document—or such a terminal loss for Mary Jane—without that hasty kidnap. Of course, it is possible that Hilda and George had to act in concert to prevent any more "trouble." Either way, this ruthless agreement removed Betty from her grandmother forever. Except for one final encounter.

"One day your adopted mother, she took you to church and she saw Grandma Blanchard there in the pews, and before the service was over she took you out of the church and home so that she wouldn't get a chance to speak to you. That was how it was. And then after that . . . nothing."

So poor Veda came face-to-face with Mary Jane in the little parish church. These two women, one with the child, the other without: a Solomonic judgment in Chapel. And Mary Jane, forced to do what seems best for Grace, must lovingly give her up. Veda and Mary Jane, the new mother, the old grandmother, both in their forties and living scarcely a mile apart, two strangers drawn together by this innocent child.

Why did Hilda give up her daughter? All accounts differ. Fanny says, "She loved you but she didn't want you growing up with the boys in the windmill." Another relative puts the onus on Grandma Blanchard: "She felt, reluctantly, that you had a better chance of education etc in a home with no other children." One of my Australian aunts writes that "Hilda let her go because growing up in that small community, they all knew. She couldn't support her daughter and didn't want her brought up in the bakery with those rough boys. George could give her an education and Veda would love her, having no child with George." My other Australian aunt believes that shame weighed heavily upon Hilda, and it was better to leave her home and family behind and try to make a new life elsewhere.

A myth overgrew this story in my mind. I came to believe, in my vilification of him, that George must have paid Hilda to go away. Thousands of people left England for Australia in the twenties and thirties. Some were children, wrenched from their parents and sent away as "orphans" to be adopted in the new world. Others took the assisted passage offered by the British government, after the 1922 Empire Land Settlement Scheme, to go out and populate the vast empty territories. I imagined that George took advantage of this scheme, as he had taken advantage of Hilda, topping up the money to send her away.

When they first met, her Australian sisters gave my mother photographs of herself at the mill, as her birthright. They move me very much. Here is Grace cuddled by her boy uncles, dandled on Grandma Blanchard's knee, danced up and down on her leg, smiling between Fred and his wife. She plays in the garden, laughs on the shore. Most uplifting is a photograph of Grace beaming up at her grandma, both perched on a knoll at Chapel beach. In every image, Mary Jane's loving eyes look down upon her.

But photographs of Grace with Hilda hardly exist. I am always distressed by this, leafing through these shots with my mother. There is one of her in Hilda's lap as a baby, but it is obscure. "What a pity my head is in so much shadow and her face isn't visible," she quietly remarks as we look at it. "The only face I really want to see is hers." In these pictures Grace appears part of a large loving family, and it brings us joy to see that she was, briefly, in her remotest past, happy. But there are no memories to buoy these images, no anecdotes to anchor them, nothing to which these scenes could be moored. She has never known anybody from this time and place and cannot feel that these images connect with the present, more than ninety years later. "It is all so far away now," she says, "that this person cannot possibly be me."

With the transcript of that first visit to Fanny there were other old papers, one of them a scrap torn from my mother's Letts diary for 1986. "Went to see Mrs. Toyne at Hogsthorpe, friend of Hilda. Says George and Hilda kept on meeting. Also her Aunt North, aged 98, aunt to Veda by marriage too, incredibly. Used to deliver milk to the mill and remembers my hair fine and fair. Also said Hilda used to meet George, putting the baby on a rug for picnics, clandestinely. This upset Grandma Blanchard."

It also upset my long-held sense of what was going on. The baby on the picnic rug was as much a shock as the village dance the night before the birth, or the unexpected arrival. Hilda couldn't possibly want to see George, an unregenerate chancer who had surely ruined her life. And yet apparently she did, bringing Grace to meet him in secret. How else could George have come to know his daughter, after all, become so possessed with claiming her?

Perhaps Hilda had some feelings for George, the sophisticated older man. I can't picture that in black and white. I only want to believe that she loved Grace, and was forced to give her up, not that she sealed it by consulting a solicitor. If there are no pictures of mother and daughter together, then surely it is only because Hilda is taking the photograph, invariably the one with the camera.

Hilda departed from my mother's life in 1929, taking that ship across the waters that circle around our world. Maybe she had hopes of return, like her brother Frank, who had gone to Melbourne before her and still come home. But the sea that connects us also separates us. Perhaps only by making this voyage could Hilda give up her child.

She left from the coast where Franklin embarked for Australia to become governor general of what is now Tasmania. A statue of him stands in the center of Hobart, an exact copy of the figure that dominates the main square in Spilsby. Franklin did not thrive in Australia and on his return to England accepted the invitation to search for the Northwest Passage. In the late summer of 1845, his convoy was sighted by Inuit whalers. Nothing more was heard of it for fourteen years. During that time more than a dozen expeditions were dispatched in search of Franklin and his men, several funded by his wife in Lincolnshire. The wreck of one of these expeditionary ships, the *Resolute*, was itself only discovered decades later; wood from its hull was used to make the Oval Office desk at which American presidents have worked ever since.

Franklin could only depart believing he would return. The party took provisions for three years, long enough to make their valiant discovery and sail back to be feted in London. But the ships were trapped in ice by 1847, and none of the crew lived to tell what happened next. Their exact fate is still disputed, though the vessels were recently discovered in eerily pristine condition on the ocean floor.

In 1926, the year of my mother's birth, headlines in the *Skegness Times* reported the discovery of a tin of meat found on a sledge abandoned by the Franklin expedition. It contained boiled beef, and when analyzed by scientists was declared to be in perfectly good condition. It is now thought that the tins contained dangerous levels of lead, which may have weakened the marines' health. In the rush to be off, the manufacturers had not tested their product, hastening these deaths in the ice.

For many years Lady Franklin refused to believe that she might be a widow. She lived and died in hope. The epitaph for Franklin's memorial in Westminster Abbey—there could be no grave—was written by her nephew-in-law, Tennyson.

Not here! The white North has thy bones: and thou,
Heroic sailor-soul,
Art passing on thine happier voyage now
Toward no earthly pole.

Sea ice grows slowly. The film of young crystals that first appears on the surface can drift there for months, keeping time with the swell; it takes several seasons to harden into pack ice. Franklin's ships moved more and more slowly as winter drew on, until they were fixed fast in the Arctic ice. And so it may be with people. My mother's feelings for her father took years to freeze into rigid aversion, and I wonder now whether they could ever be melted. When I showed her George's radiant photograph of Veda in the kitchen in Bradford, speaking of its beauty and grace, she could not believe that he had taken it.

15

Grandparents

I should have had a grandfather, except that he died a decade before I was born. I would like to have studied his face, circled in his embrace, like the child in Ghirlandaio's masterpiece. *Old Man and His Grandson* is a picture of tenderness between two generations who have not the friction of being so close in age as parents and children. The old man with the carbuncled nose looks down at the flawless boy, who returns his gaze with the same unhurried interest. The child's gaze (and the picture) invite you to imagine the surface of that nose, the feel of its bulbous swellings; but the child's love (and the picture) cancel those deformities. This is how it should be between grandparent and grandchild: mutual curiosity, unqualified love.

I never heard anything good about George from my mother, beyond the things he made and a few childhood games. From all the other fragments I could find, I fixed upon a single story. George was an ill-tempered, aggressive, domineering older man who seduced a very much younger woman and insisted on taking the daughter born of that deed. He imprisoned the child as far as he was able, first in the house, then the post office, until someone recognized her artistic gifts and pride so overcame his possessiveness that he set her free to study art. He dies; she shuts her eyes. Extinction, followed by oblivion.

George Maybrook Elston: a pompous signature and a handful of photographs, a memory of gaiety at the Vine, where he plays the drums in that modest band, and of angry outbursts and ferocious coughing at home. Of course he is more than just this. I can hardly bear to think of the way he cheated and confined my mother, but we are not the collected memories of other people. I must be able to

look more steadily at George, as his grandchild, consider the linea-
ments of his life: the nonexistent father and the sudden orphaning
at thirteen, when he no longer belongs to anyone; the uprooting
from Yorkshire on a branch-line train down through England to
the port of Plymouth to set sail for South Africa, a land scarcely
mentioned or known to his contemporaries before the Boer War. In
Plymouth he signs up with other raw recruits for a conflict so
remote as to be unimaginable. G. M. Elston, nineteen years old,
Signaller 24154, 11th (Yorkshire) Company, 3rd Battalion of the
Imperial Yeomanry. There was no conscription; he didn't have to
go. A hazy photograph survives of him leading a little band of men
down a hill to the Battle of Tygerfontein, armed with nothing but
the mirrors with which they flashed messages across the hot valleys.
Whatever lay before him in England was replaced by this new life
of danger, of stalled days and sudden mobilizations, parched canvas, exhausted horses, and disease. The draftsmanship praised by
Rebe may not have its expression in anything that survives, but the
army recognized his gifts, awarding him a distinction for engineer-
ing drawing. His career was surely one of decline thereafter—glory
in the Eastern Cape more qualified in the Great War, where he is
invalided out by his bronchitis; prowess in drawing followed by a
downward spiral through the 1920s, the General Strike, and the
Depression, holding tight to a job of ever-dwindling importance.

From the Cape he returns to Hull, and a position selling lubricating oil for machines, his wartime expertise no doubt respected. Then swiftly on to Bradford, where he meets Veda, and they shift from the Midlands city to this coastal village that is home to her but so inconveniently remote for his work; although that might have its appeal. George is always moving, restless, even before he becomes a soap salesman; three more decades of traveling follow. I have a handful of his train tickets from the 1920s, expenses penciled on the back in his immaculate script. The routes are planned, the possibilities evaluated before every departure, his successes—and failures—recorded in the all-important order book, a measure of the pressures upon him. The soap he sells will gradually become redundant as chemists devise ever-more-potent detergents. His customers in the dark satanic mills are always the same, never increasing in number. It must have been a Sisyphean task to fill that book.

Once, George picked up a boy who was dithering by the tide and threw him straight into the water. *Get on with it!* This is told in a letter to my mother by the nephew who was banished to bed for bringing home the wrong cigarettes. I think of George raging at poor Granny Crawford. These incidents are so easily imagined they spring into my head fully formed, graphic as recurrent nightmares. I recoil from them almost more than from events I cannot so readily picture: the affair with Hilda, the betrayal of Veda, the lies he told his daughter. These are, for the moment, still obscure. Historians tell of redemption: the addict who went to Australia and became a war hero; the adulterer who founded a children's hospital. I want to find George's better nature, to see him like the grandfather in the painting, with the innocent love of a grandchild.

His intentions must be apparent, at least, in what he made—the doll's house, the bookcases, the photograph of Veda. The fine Edwardian aviary for birds in the garden, above all the theater with its potential for the full Shakespearean repertoire. And when George hands Betty the Bible that Christmas Day, solemnly declaring that it is the most important book she will ever own, shame might prompt the rhetoric. Even my mother considered this possibility in her memoir: "At this distance in time, I can see that he was perhaps in the throes of everlasting guilt over my advent. He was also a sick man, bedevilled increasingly by recurrent bronchitis every winter, and lumbago which literally doubled him over. A teenager enjoying robust health myself, and having no idea of the effects of ill-health upon the temper, I found his incessant coughing a great trial. But my mother was of such good nature she could only have been sympathetic."

Bent double also by his weekly suitcase, lugged around the country until retirement. And George does not retire until he is sixty-six, the year my mother comes of age. He has to keep earning to pay for his late-life daughter. The child might not appreciate this—*I never asked to be born*—but the grandchild does. His wages were smaller every year. I found a newspaper ad in which he puts his bandsman's costume up for sale: "In fine condition, little used in recent years." He was only fifty-five.

Again and again I return to the photograph of Veda: the beauty of the image, the love of the woman, the gentle light streaming through the scene and his camera. Time is photography's true subject, people always say, but this picture seems alive to the stranger phenomenon of chance, the immense lucky strike by which two people meet and fall in love.

A lifetime of anger towards George has washed out to sea. I have grown up and learned about human frailty; the effects of foolishness and disappointment; the longing for a child. I can imagine what it is to go out the front door and leave one's mistakes behind; the newness of Monday, its redemptive return to work, the canceling out of one week's failures by the arrival of the next; the limitless, ever-changing world seen from trains and through travel. And what was Hilda at first but a bright new traveling companion, going forward together with George? She shared what homebound Veda never could.

And who am I to know what the wager was in the end: whether Betty was the solace for a lost relationship with Hilda, or the adoption an act of expiation towards his daughter and her very young mother? Perhaps he gave Veda the child she could not have to atone for his infidelity; or perhaps he actually loved Betty. George struggles so hard to control the world, but cannot. His great idea, to pass my mother off as born to the Elstons, is as much a disaster as his later pretense that she is not his natural child. He gambles with the truth, twice, and falls to his fate by the water.

But I have been angry with them all on behalf of my mother. Even Hilda, poor Hilda, with a desperate pregnancy at twenty, her life irrevocably altered, no choice available in those days: How could she involve herself in all this swithering and then end it with a complete renunciation of Grace, especially when her own family so loves and wants this child? Why is it Mary Jane and not Hilda who returns for Betty that day? And how can Hilda be party to a legal document that is effectively a restraining order against her own mother and all the Blanchards? When the document is signed, Hilda maintains this secrecy long after George's death, reported to her in Australia. If she confided in her husband, they must have made a pact not to tell their children, for Hilda obviously kept her first daughter a secret from Judy and Susan all through their successive sojourns in England, when they were within hailing distance of Betty. Shame does not explain everything, nor does George's insistent campaigning, or even the general principle of confidentiality in adoption. But every act is human here; nothing is beyond imagination or understanding.

Answers to some of these questions came from several members of the Blanchard family to whom my mother wrote in the 1980s. They are so tender, these missives sent to a woman who might as well have been a stranger. But in fact they all knew of her existence. Each correspondent in turn is amazed to learn that Betty knows nothing about her past; and each goes on to give a different version of the story.

One second cousin writes to explain that Fred Blanchard—"a lovely kind gentleman with twinkling blue eyes, a warden of Hogsthorpe church"—was unable to live with the shameful situation. Some believe that Fred and Mary Jane together urged Hilda to give up her child, though this is surely contradicted by the kidnap. Still others repeat the claim that the mill was too rough a place to raise Grace, or emphasize the social advantages offered by George: a quiet and more studious house, a better school for Betty, possibly even a girls' school, though this is obviously not what happened. Indeed, there is much talk of education as the main argument for the adoption, which makes little sense considering that Hilda herself was a boarder at Louth Grammar. I sieve the evidence like flour. Nobody explicitly mentions reputation, or marriage prospects, or seduction or anything so coarse. But each correspondent seems equally surprised by my mother's ignorance.

This secrecy makes me want to scream, like my mother trapped in the Edinburgh lift. How was she supposed to know anything about her past if they all kept mute? George died in 1952. Grandma Blanchard lived on for another seventeen years knowing where Betty was, sending cuttings about her out to Australia—school, art college, graduation, marriage, even my brother's birth—so that Hilda knew too. Were they just abiding by a worthless document all that time? There had been no legal threat whatsoever since my mother came of age in 1947. The unending silence may have been out of respect for Hilda, Veda, Betty, or all three; or for the sake of George's *amour propre*. Yet there was little point in it ever since the day Aunt Emma unleashed her revelation, backed up by a photograph, on that green country bus. Whatever the original motive, it must surely have changed over time until everyone thought it was just too late.

And even when the wall came down in 1986, the same thing seemed to happen in miniature during the family gatherings with Judy and Susan. Hardly anything was said about Hilda, her character, her feelings, what her life was like with and without Grace, or Betty, still less how (or when) that name could have been so casually changed. My mother never asked Veda about the adoption, the sudden arrival of this child in her house; and I can never ask George. I marvel that she knows so little about her father and that I have to dig so deep. A great silence hangs over Chapel.

I could place too much emphasis on George's end simply because I have a death certificate: shortest of stories, last tale of cause and effect. Even a birth certificate may not give us so much. Of Ghirlandaio, poignant painter, we have neither a month nor a year for his birth, sometime in the fifteenth century, only the narrative of his very sudden illness, carried off by "a pestilential fever" in his forties. George's death certificate—which of course my mother does not have, so I send off for it—tells a sad story. He dies at home on Valentine's Day, at the age of seventy-one. Mrs. Simpson has come round from next door, presumably to comfort Veda, since Betty is not there. Dr. Paterson certifies his old friend's death. The cause is that annual bronchitis Betty found so hard to endure, which has finally turned into hypostatic pneumonia. George is described, here, in this last of all documents, simply as Traveller.

Books are reckonings. I picture an encounter with my grandfather in the afterlife, should it exist. The child's question immediately presents itself: What age are we in that state? Is it the age at which we die? In which case my mother is now twenty-two years older than George was at his death; old enough to be his mother, in this existential algebra. Perhaps George is young again and yet to make his fateful mistake; or seventy-one and furious to find the past revived. Maybe he explains it all to me as nobody else ever could: grandfather to grandchild, patient, loving, with an eternity of time to explain the vagaries of life.

My mother says George had no accent, and I see him slipping free of the Yorkshire tones he was born to, always escaping the status quo. And though he is my grandfather, and I have his blood, he is like all long-distant ancestors to me—these people of the past who elude us, no matter how hard we try to drag them back out of time's tide. A photograph and an anecdote or two; if we are lucky, some writing or a headstone.

If he could be brought back from beyond the bar, what would George say? That he had no regrets, that he'd had the joy of a child and known what it was to love Betty as well as Veda (and perhaps Hilda)? Or would he say that nobody understood him, all the decades of hard grind up and down the country, the misery of having no child followed by the ingratitude of the one who came, and then went? Shut down the heart, remain fiercely practical.

I have another grandfather whom I also did not know, on my father's side. He died running for a bus at fifty. But he lives on in people's conversations—always cracking jokes, the life and soul, the man who built the first crystal radio in Dunfermline and turned the volume so high they could hear Caruso singing *Tosca* on the far side of town. Willie Cumming's warmth survives in words. George Elston seems to die by them.

Yet I know he had friends and drinking partners, conducted his fellow musicians at dances. Mr. Geo. Elston officiated, it says in newspaper accounts of fund-raisers for the cottage hospital. He wins a dance competition himself, surely taught by his mother, Lauretta. An ex-serviceman, he continues to serve, a mender, a carpenter, an engineer, a signalman in the Home Guard. His precision is there in the perfect point of that ancient pencil. I can imagine so much more, but my sense is that George does not want my attention. The subterfuge is his idea; he is the founder of all this silence, as averted as Count Bellelli in Degas's painting.

Historians do not give much consideration to the feelings of people in the past: emotions are to be avoided as unstable, irrelevant, or simply unverifiable in the absence of documentary evidence. A teacher at my school once gave a lesson about the naming of sixteenth-century children—how each new baby might be christened John, even if it was a girl, because infant mortality rates were so high and the ancestral name must be preserved; this was supposedly proof that the parents felt no grief. We learned that widows conveniently wed their neighbors, widowers married their wives' sisters, that half-wit children were suppressed, and all of it with nothing but brutal pragmatism. As a student, I remember a professor insisting that romantic love did not exist until the Renaissance, when it was invented; that mothers and fathers did not develop parental feelings for their young until it was obvious that they would survive infancy; and other contrived academic hypotheses. Only consider Dante's love songs to Beatrice, or Ben Jonson's lament for his beloved son, dead at seven, his best and most feeling-ful poetry. Even now, art historians regard Ghirlandaio's painting of 1491 as an anomaly because it runs against their theories of Renaissance portraiture in acknowledging the old man's deformity. I have even read that it must be an imaginary portrait, devised to illustrate the blindness of a grandchild's love. It is amazing that any scholar should be so arrogant as to assume a lack of feeling in the long dead simply because there is no textual evidence of the oppo-site. Or that anyone could look at the Ghirlandaio and not see a portrait of two people who really lived, and loved, not see the authenticity of both the likeness and the emotion represented there. Look at the photograph of Betty and Mary Jane on the beach; it is exactly the same relationship.

My mother's childhood was given to me as a black-and-white fable, and I am trying to confuse it with color. I cannot bear to think that it was all so straightforward, or that they all suffered so much—Hilda bereft and banished, Grandma Blanchard heartbroken, Veda presumably flattened, my mother lied to and deprived of her free-dom, my grandfather loathed and forgotten. George gave me my mother, loved Veda, was drawn to Hilda, whose daughters adored her as a woman of utmost patience and kindness. All around us are stories that cannot be squared or circled or turned into something so easily defined. Death, after all, comes to interrupt any narrative that looks as if it might have the audacity to try to complete itself.

The cortège passes through the market square, past the statue of vanished Franklin, and into the graveyard at Spilsby, where George himself disappears.

From him my mother inherited a perfect sense of rhythm on the drums, and possibly her gift for drawing, although I never understand why this is regarded as such a heritable trait; we do not expect builders, dentists, or composers to hand down professional genes. From Hilda, she inherited prodigiously flexible thumbs, as demonstrated in a photograph of her with some newly discovered Blanchard relatives all miming in a row. The picture immediately tells you that they are related: biological proof. But what else do they share? In the ninety-two years of my mother's lifetime the nature–nurture debate has flourished, but it is as if she exists beyond the influence of either. She has her social fears and her double-jointed thumbs, she still loves jam tarts and encourages my children to make them. But so what? Without any pattern, she turned herself into an ideal mother, a tender grandmother. She alone invented herself.

Go your own way. That was my father's exhortation. He said it often, and it has been the inspiration of my life. He lived it, and so did my mother in her more reticent way, even from an early age. Lately a letter was returned to her by an old school friend. It follows a chance encounter between them on the train from Lincoln to Mumby Road. Betty is twenty. She is responding to the resentful suggestion that she has gotten above herself and betrayed her origins, going off to art college. She writes with such modesty about all the things she is experiencing for the first time: the exhilaration of music, newspapers, comedies on radio and screen, the humor of James Thurber, the novels of D. H. Lawrence and Graham Greene, the cartoons of H. M. Bateman, Renaissance painting, Degas, dancing with boys, staying up all night talking or drawing, having a room of her own. I see my young mother go forward, making herself up as she goes.

She gave me the only grandparent I ever knew, sweet-faced Veda. A photograph of her from 1902 shows an Edwardian girl wearing a waist-length gold chain. I have the picture, the chain, and its box, which still holds something of her—a breath, a faint dust—in its faded silk lining. All enter into living color for me because I knew Veda. I can still see her bent hands, and hear the slight burr on the *r* as she tells my brother and me not to quarrel. I know that she had rhotacism, and that this is an element of herself as much as her fondness for handkerchiefs embroidered with pansies or for simnel cake, a thing as antique to me as the cartwheel pies in a Brueghel.

She sits with us children at the table, smiling even though she is quite deaf and cannot hear what we are saying. She goes about tidying, shoulders hunched, frail body kept warm with many layers of wool. She holds up the blue glass to the light, thin arm around me, fine hair caught up in a nearly invisible net, the half-smile about her mouth completed in her fine blue eyes. And when she dies, I dream that she is standing by the garden gate, still smiling, but her eyes have turned into the amber beads of her necklace.

Somehow she found another small community late in life, among the congregation of the Scottish church across the road, at the infirmary where she spent afternoons sewing with like-minded ladies. She kept working away, long after George's death, holding up her spirits. Had she long ago forgiven him, or mildly accepted her fate? I might guess both.

One last photograph, in sixties Kodachrome, shows Veda at the kitchen table in Edinburgh. She is seated before a birthday cake, made by Mother, with a constellation of candles. She looks down at my brother's upturned face with such tenderness. It is another Ghirlandaio.

I look at that picture again, and realize with a start that I am not related to this grandmother by blood, unlike Hilda Blanchard. But that means nothing at all. What matters is my strange inability to think of Hilda as my grandparent in the first place; for me that role seems to skip a generation, back to Mary Jane Blanchard.

Ever since I learned that it was she who took Betty off the sands, my heart has gone out to this woman who lost her daughter to Australia and her granddaughter to a man she hoped would keep away. How hard she tried to bring Betty back; how much she longed to see her once more. And it might have happened, if not for this self-sustaining silence that continued for decades, long after the adoption agreement was null and void. Betty could have found the windmill and met Mary Jane; she could have discovered the whereabouts of her birth mother—and vice versa. But they were all paralyzed, frozen, my mother too, immobile as figures in a picture. The local people looked away. The plowmen all plowed on.

16

The Windmill

On the eve of the Second World War, one of Fred Blanchard's workmen climbed up inside the windmill when nobody was about and nailed a bag to the uppermost beam. The following morning he left Lincolnshire for the army, quite possibly never to return. First he was posted to France, later Italy and North Africa, in the blazing heat of the long desert war. He did not see the village of Hogsthorpe again for six years, one hundred and sixty-one days. During this immense span of time, the young soldier often remembered his bag and wondered what anyone would think if they came across its secret contents, especially if he never came home.

The bag contained an agricultural thermometer, some stones, and a black-and-white photograph of a car. This car could have been any car, ordinary as thousands of others, except that the image singled it out. The stones could have come from any beach, and the thermometer was of the heavy metal variety commonly used on farms for forcing mushrooms. There was nothing specific or special about any of these things to a stranger's eye, although together they cried out for interpretation. But for the workman they spoke of a shared past: mementos of time spent with Hilda Blanchard.

Objects mean more than they are, signify more than themselves. One man's chaff is another man's treasure. A stone is easy: it might recall a walk. A car could be a haven for two. But the thermometer would have foxed anyone. It is an odd thing, terminally rusted yet still quick with mercury, apparently defunct yet suddenly alive when out in the sun. It sits on the desk before me now, along with Tennyson's box, and the photograph of the little girl among the tulips. They all mean far more than they are.

Hilda had come back to Hogsthorpe in 1938, this time without Lance but bringing four-year-old Judy. She stayed at the mill for many months, teaching in the local school, helping in the bakery. And it was here that she met Paul Eresby, her father's best baker, who arrived at five every morning, put on his whites, and began the first dough for the bread. He was there for long hours each day, moving around the mill and the kitchen. They became close. The stones in the bag were gathered with her on Chapel Sands. The thermometer was for taking the temperature of the soil in which they grew mushrooms, raising a crop of white caps together out of humid darkness. The photograph shows the car in which Paul taught Hilda to drive in the lanes around Hogsthorpe and Chapel.

The shot is so humble—just an unremarkable old heap pulled up by a hedge—that its significance couldn't possibly be to do with the car itself. It is still in the small brown envelope in which it was sent with utmost sensitivity to give some comfort to my mother.

Ever since she heard Fanny tell the story of her birth, the memory of Hilda's outburst to the doctor continued to lacerate my mother. Her adult self understood the despair, the ordeal of concealment through nine months, and the terrible exposure on that August day. But the child in her still grieved. It did not seem that George had wanted her to the point of love, only ownership; it did not seem as if Hilda could have cared for her quite enough to keep her. And all the recent generosity shown by the surviving members of the Blanchard family implying that she had been loved as a child established nothing but the fact of their kindness. The photographs of her early years at the mill did not persuade her, then or since. But then came a letter with a Hogsthorpe postmark in the first week of 1987.

Dear Betty, Mrs. Cumming,

I've found out your address, you don't know me, but I thought I'd better write. I was told you'd been to the village looking for news about your real mother. I've written before but tore them up, too much to put in a letter. But I'll send this one and hope it helps. When you were a baby I knew all about you, you were Hilda Blanchard's daughter Grace. They say your name got changed to Betty when you were three and she gave you up to the father. You must be 60 thereabouts now, but I only knew you as a child, every day except Sundays for those 3 years. What it is you ought to know—you WAS wanted. I'm telling you this in case you ever thought different. Hilda couldn't keep you, see, in them times it was hard and she didn't want you brought up with boys, 4 brothers she had. She went to Australia after. If you come again to Hogsthorpe there's questions I could answer if you wanted. Yours truly Paul Eresby. I was with the Blanchard family in those days, hired hand in the mill.

My mother was startled to receive this letter. Apart from Fanny, everyone who had ever seen Hilda with Grace was long since dead, or so she thought. But here was a living witness who could testify to the relationship between mother and daughter. She returned to Hogsthorpe to visit Paul Eresby, who was himself surprised to set

eyes on her again after almost sixty years. Her presence filled him
with renewed sorrow for them both, as it seems to me, and the
other lives that they might both have led. It seemed impossible for
either of them to breach the social meniscus; they did not weep, or
reach out towards one another, or even speak deeply of Hilda. I do
not think that this was just propriety, although Mr. Eresby had
long ago married and had children of his own. Perhaps there was a
loyalty—towards Hilda, towards Veda. But my mother wrote a
note of the conversation in her Letts diary that day—"Grace
adopted after pressure from George, kidnapped by Mary Jane,
Fanny and third sister Emma. The sisters want her back. Grandma
Blanchard was tiny! Memory of her crying in the bakehouse, Paul
upset himself. George and Hilda keep in touch. Hilda erratic, distressed, throwing an inkwell." If only there was more; the scenes are
so dramatically abrupt. But once they had met, it seemed possible
for Paul and Elizabeth to write to each other, and there were several
more letters.

For my mother these are perhaps the clearest proof she will ever
have of Hilda's feelings for her. One was written in April: "Spring
with things coming to life, lambs, calves etc being born, should be
a joyous time, not bring sadness. But it reminds me of an evening I
was teaching your mother to drive. She pulled up to let a pheasant
and chicks cross the road. It upset her so much, that I had to drive

her home. Her thoughts turned to you." Another tells of Hilda trying to see her daughter on the beach, and standing in vain in front
of George's house. A third describes an afternoon in which Hilda
tries to get a letter by a back route to her child—he does not divulge
how—and asks Paul to send it. To his eternal shame, he foolishly
asks to read it first; she weeps, he tries to console her; the letter is
never sent. And even now, half a century later, Paul agonizes about
writing all this to Grace, as she still is to him.

I promised all those years ago that Hilda could talk to me
with the sure knowledge that I would in no circumstances
betray her trust. After some soul searching I have come to the
conclusion that she would forgive me for speaking. I am not
sure that you were completely satisfied that your mother really
wanted you so I have put pen to paper now to try and convince you that this was the case. You poor little innocent baby,
in a few months you had entered and affected many people's
lives. For most it was heartbreak. It should never have been
handled the way it was. Those principally concerned soon
arrived at that conclusion but it was too late, even so, they
made a futile grab to get you back before breaking the law.
Mr. and Mrs. Blanchard were regular church goers, pillars of
the church in fact. They could not stand the shame, he being

a friend of the vicar. Under this pressure they made a decision they were soon to regret. They drove their daughter to a land twelve thousand miles away and lost her forever, and missed the joy in seeing their two lovely grand daughters grow up. Mrs. Blanchard never gave up hope that one day she and Hilda would be reunited to be parted no more. She thought it had been brought about when Hilda's husband agreed to come and work at the bakery. Her happiness was short lived. Lance soon wanted to return to Australia. In Hogsthorpe churchyard there was a vacant spot for Hilda in the curbed section where Mr. and Mrs. Blanchard are at rest with Arthur and Frank. The churchyard is now closed.

Paul Eresby is the only correspondent who ever met George.

Your father was an extremely intelligent man. But domineering and somewhat like a character from Dickens. I thought if you were under his influence too long you would be sour and unapproachable. I am glad I was wrong in my assumption. I too wish you had met your mother and grandparents. With hindsight I think we ought to have brought this about. What seemed right at the time now appears cruel and inhuman. You say Hilda must have found happiness with her two daughters.

In my opinion not complete. How can you explain that with Judy nearly four years old she was begging to have you pointed out so she could see you. Could she have been contented with a look? We shall never know, but the chance should have been taken. I think after reading this you should realise that what you suffered would have to be multiplied by two to be anywhere near what your mother went through, and went on twice as long for if you have grown up children you were not so old when you found happiness.

Eresby says that Hilda simply could not keep her child; yet he also implies that her parents' shame was decisive. These accounts are not necessarily contradictory. His feeling for Hilda leads him to an emotional reckoning—it was much worse for Hilda than for the child she abandoned—that hurt my mother at that time, but his loyalty to the Blanchards is undivided. Immense compassion for Hilda does not stop him from feeling the same for Mary Jane. "Hilda had three lovely daughters and I am glad to have met you all. Your happy ending was a long time coming. But Mrs. Blanchard was like a second mother to me and in this desperate tale, she suffered most, reaching the age of ninety. If in unburdening myself I have caused you more pain I am truly sorry, but remember I have had this to myself for fifty years and confided in no one."

* * *

I have grown to feel this way too; to wonder whether Mary Jane lost most—a daughter as well as a granddaughter, outliving her husband and two of her sons. I could not bear to think that she never saw Grace again. But with the notes of the encounter with Fanny I have now found something else: an old reel-to-reel recording that none of us had ever played; my mother was too sad to listen, and eventually, I suppose, the technology became obsolete. I bless the Blanchards for giving us these four minutes of revelation.

The sound was recorded by one of Grandma Blanchard's sons, Hugh, on Christmas Day 1965. They are trying out their new machine. Reel one is a sea of voices, all talking over each other, and off-mike, mainly about presents and visitors and seasonal subjects. I feel overwhelmed with the desire to rescue Mary Jane's voice from this tide, to identify even one syllable spoken by her, and imagine taking the tape to some forensic lab and paying any price to distinguish the sound of my great-grandmother, her being momentarily incarnated. I can hear an aged voice murmuring in the background for a second or two. Then nothing. But in reel two she is right there on her own, answering occasional questions. Hers is a soft soprano, with a melodic laugh covering up the self-consciousness she feels on hearing that she is being recorded on this cumbersome machine for posterity. The tape runs out after a couple of minutes, but it is long enough to hear her tender tones to all involved, her sweetness of character. She speaks so lovingly to her grown-up sons, now grandparents themselves, and remarks, almost as if talking about the weather, that she is blind nowadays. And then, just before the tape runs out, she pictures the lifeboat at Chapel and how they used to take it out on the sea for fun even when there was no call for it. And she is struggling to remember the name of her great friend there, all those times with her, and it turns out to be George Stow's wife at Stow's Stores. She always went visiting Mrs. Stow down the lane, she says. Mary Jane must have known exactly how my mother was getting on, what she looked like, perhaps even how she spoke, through this lifelong friendship. She must have seen Grace in that very same place, framed behind the post-office counter.

Words and images. In life as in art we do not always see what is going on at the edges, or even the foreground, do not notice what seems irrelevant or superfluous to our needs and theories. Perception is guided by our own priorities. Five hundred years ago, Brueghel played upon our habits of looking, knowing that we would be a good while pondering the plowman, the sun, sea, and ship, before we ever got to the shepherd staring up at the sky and realized that there must be something else going on, finally spotting the shock of Icarus.

Among the photographs that came from Australia was the very picture of the little girl among the tulips that always stood by Hilda's bed. On the back is written, in my aunt Judy's hand, "Betty in the orchard at Grandma Blanchard's mill. She was still Grace. This is before the kidnap." My mother is certainly surrounded by trees, and she looks as happy as in all the other mill photographs; I have always regarded it as a bittersweet vision of paradise lost. There she is in her best dress, with its pleats and pearl buttons and that long chain of beads, shining hair and matching smile, out among the tulips and trees. But look closer, look again; this is what I should have told myself. The tulips tell us that this is spring, probably April or May, given the lilies of the valley and the fact that she is not wearing a coat. If Betty is still at the mill, then it must be 1929, in which case she would be two years old. But the girl in this picture is clearly three, rising to four, definitely conversational, quite possibly on the way to reading. In which case it can only be the spring of 1930, after the kidnap, by which time she has been living with George and Veda for at least six months. This is not the mill, therefore, and my sense is that it is in fact the land around 1 St. Leonard's Villas. Other photographs from the Elston album at this time show the same landscape, the same beads and dress.

The photographer is not Hilda, Mary Jane, or any of the Blanchards. It is George.

The fringe Betty has in the mill pictures has grown out, her hair now pinned neatly to one side for this formal occasion. George has posed his daughter with particular care, so that she appears ringed by trees and spring flowers. She is following his instructions with enthusiasm, standing at a jaunty angle, hand on hip as if dancing, holding a bright smile for his camera—and the viewer for whom the image is intended. It is a declaration, almost a kind of propaganda.

George takes the picture, and makes an unusually large print which he sends, along with another of Betty surrounded by several new toys, pleasingly configured by height, all the way to Australia. Both portraits are composed specially for Hilda, and the perfect size for framing. The tulip scene still bears the rusty imprint of her bedside frame. Betty is well; all is well. Here is the ocular proof: a beautifully dressed, well-nourished, reassuringly happy child. Everyone else may be sworn to silence, but George and Hilda are in touch through images.

The photograph tells me this, but it has quite another meaning to my mother. It is important to her because she knows that this is how Hilda continued to see her lost daughter on the other side of the world. Towards the end of the birthday memoir, she suddenly falters, wondering with characteristic humility why I wanted her to write the story of what she calls her insignificant life; then she is struck by the idea that she could at least justify it as an act of gratitude for the happy days with her parents. These appear to me so few that the debt is surely exorbitantly overpaid. Still, they must have occurred, I tell myself, because the photographs say it is so. And then I remember that even when posing in the tree with the *Happy Days* annual, she tells of feeling the opposite emotion. I cannot be sure that Betty is as merry among the tulips as she seems; perhaps I need words, after all.

Hilda kept the photograph by her forever. "A picture of a little girl who once belonged to me," as she described it to Susan. It reminds me of my mother's phrase: "You are my most precious possession." I did not understand it, still react against its connotations of ownership, until I remember its corollary: "I never belonged to anyone until I belonged to you." Once, she wrote a letter to the grandfather she never knew, Fred Blanchard, in which she speaks of being disowned. It is the language of the period, but also of the heart. *You are mine, I am yours*; and so we still say.

But that is not how any of them talked to her. Nobody ever spoke of love, a word Betty never heard in childhood. Even now she has only modest hopes of other people's affections. She is the woman who always asks all the questions of egotists who never offer any in return, who writes back to every letter by return of post, who cannot let gratitude be delayed by a moment, who never wants anyone to be left out, sincere in all her love and concern. Two things are very often said of her: that she takes self-deprecation almost to an art form, and that she can charm the birds from the trees. Where others would be hurt by the coldness of this world, in response to such charm, she takes it as normal. Her childhood diminished any sense of expectation.

It is all as remote as a fairy tale for my mother, but not for me. I reach back for my forebears, longing to make them love her. For most of my life, the only childhood photographs of her were those taken by George. Given what I knew about these years, I would look at them as if the roles were reversed: How can I reach you, dear child to whom I feel so maternal, how can I protect you from what is coming next, when you will no longer belong to anyone? I can't pluck you out of these old images, fading away even as your life is drawing to its close. I cannot give you back the lost happiness. How many years before anybody said they loved you?

The first inkling of that love, for me, came not in words but images: the photographs sent to my mother by the Australian Blanchards. These pictures were not in albums, but loose. They came in a plastic bag, a scattering of shadows from the past. Mary Jane dandling her. Hugh and Frank holding her hands. Grandma and grandchild on the beach. But lately I wrote to my aunts, searching for more answers, and in return came a package from Australia containing several photographs of George with Grace before she was Betty. He is kissing her, kneeling with her in the shallow waters in long-legged swimming costumes, monkeying about on the shore. There are many of her at the mill, playing on the doorstep, feeding chickens. But the shock is a picture I already know very well: George holding Grace on Chapel Sands.

The moment is gone, passed into fading history, and yet something pulls it forward out of monochrome. For now we are back upon the beach and nothing bad has happened yet. My mother has not been handed over to George, lost Hilda, been kidnapped, or even shifted from Grace to Betty. Time runs backwards, and here she is once more before her life divides. I look for the spark of chance, that trace of the here and now that the photographer cannot control, and it is there in that almost imperceptible blur of motion. We look back into the past to see the origins of the future. And it is as if the photograph predicts that future: my mother shifts in George's grasp, trying to go her own way.

The photograph implies the photographer; until now I could only guess who this was. Turning the scene around in the mind's eye, and knowing to whom it belonged, I see George looking back at Hilda.

The three of them are together like any other family on the beach, and Hilda is taking the photograph with George's camera. It is better than the one they have at the mill. She stands quite close to Grace and George to frame the scene, but more telling than this intimacy is the expression on his face. This is the only family photograph in which George smiles.

The moustache of his Bradford days has gone, along with some of his hair. The face is thinner, older, gentler. The photograph has not altered since I first saw it with the eyes of a child, but my understanding of it has changed, just like the Chapel stories my mother used to tell; I see it all anew.

It is a way of keeping them all together, this picture, like the one my mother took of her parents in the garden; and perhaps it is elegiac, Hilda taking up the camera to commemorate these last days on Chapel Sands, knowing that her daughter may soon be gone. But my sense is that it comes before all of the sorrow and confusion and is a bright souvenir of that day, skimmed like the day itself out of time.

George made one copy for himself and another for Hilda; that much is clear. But there is a difference between them. The print that stayed in Chapel was entirely mute and obscure, hidden in the back of the family album. The other one is not silent. Written across the top in fountain pen is this declaration: we love you.

Sending it to me, my Australian aunt was puzzled. Who could have written these words, to whom were they addressed? She was not sure, for the simple reason that she had never seen George's handwriting. And it is a revelation of another kind for me too, for I hear my grandfather's voice for the first and only time. All I ever had of him were a few stories and some photographs, but now came the speech of his heart. Looking again at the family album, I realize that almost the only person in it is his child, again and again, and that George cannot appear for taking her picture. But now they are together, father and daughter bound forever in this image, and speaking these words to the third, to the lost mother—we love you.

ACKNOWLEDGMENTS

This book is written out of love for my mother, whose truest name was Grace. She gave me everything through our lives together. This is the least I can give back to a woman whose idea of a birthday present for her child was not to buy a memoir but to write one especially for her. And then to give that daughter permission to use it, so generously, thirty years later. Grace, Betty, beloved Elizabeth: my gratitude is unending.

To all those who gave me the chance to tell this tale, I offer heartfelt thanks. To my great friend Patrick Walsh, best of all agents, who so well understood why I wanted to construct a pedestal for my mother's writing. To Nan Graham of Scribner, who so appreciated it and sent her praise all the way from Sixth Avenue to a rural cottage in Wiltshire, where my mother was astonished to receive it in her ninety-second year. And to her colleague Daniel Loedel, for his acute and sensitive editing and his faith in the enterprise.

At Chatto, my thanks to Kathryn Fry for her eagle-eyed copy-editing, Kris Potter for his vision of Chapel on the cover, to productive Polly Collier, and marvelous Mia Quibell-Smith. Clara Farmer, editorial director of Chatto and Windus, once asked me to write about my sense of art as vital to life itself, and not a thing apart, and this is the second time I have written that book by other means and she has not complained. For her outstanding editorial rigor, her meticulous intellect and eye, I thank her.

I wondered for a long time precisely how George took the photograph of Veda in the kitchen. I am very grateful to the photographer Peter Cattrell for his wisdom about period images and cameras; and to Z, clandestine operative in Maryland, whose knowledge of reconnaissance photography taught me so much. Thanks to Simon Bradley, renowned railway historian, for his help with the complexities of the Mablethorpe Loop. And to Tom Ambridge and his siblings for allowing me to quote from May Hill's compelling Chapel war diaries.

My dear Australian aunts, Susan Baker and Judith Beale, have been kindness itself, answering questions, sending revelatory photographs, and suffering my suggestions. I hope they will forgive my interpretation of events that took place before we were born. This tale of our forebears is for their children, too, and for my brother Timothy Cumming, whose dynamism helped us all to find each other in the first place. And it is for Hilda Blanchard's great-grandchildren in England: Ruby and Holly Cumming, and my adored daughters, Hilla and Thea Sewell.

The writing of *On Chapel Sands* was sustained by friends so modest they probably do not even know how or that they helped: Sarah Baxter, Julian Bell, Marcel Berlins, Patricia Carrott, Louise Cattrell, Jill Chisholm, Kate Colquhoun, David Cox, Sarah Donaldson, Lisa Forrell, Kate Kellaway, Carol McDaid, Alex McLennan, Louise Swan, William Sewell, Ruth Williamson, the late Bronwen Pulsford, and Marion Owen. I still remember the exhilarating conversations I had with Tom Lubbock about some of these pictures when he was alive, and I was privileged to know him.

Dennis Sewell has lived with this book closer than anyone, turning it over with me day after day, never ceasing in his abundant generosity. His compassion always produces new insights. For this, as for everything he does to help me, to help us, boundless gratitude and love.